CHARLES L. THOMPSON AND ASSOCIATES ARKANSAS ARCHITECTS 1885-1938

F. HAMPTON ROY

EDITOR: RALPH J. MEGNA

Published in cooperation with the
QUAPAW QUARTER ASSOCIATION
Little Rock, Arkansas

AUGUST HOUSE
Little Rock

Dedicated to those individuals, companies, and institutions who commissioned the design of the buildings described in this book, as well as to those who have lovingly cared for them since their construction.

ISBN 0-935304-50-9

Library of Congress Catalog Card Number: 82-73554

Roy, F. Hampton
Charles L. Thompson and Associates
Little Rock: August House
128 p.

First printing: January 1983

TABLE OF CONTENTS

ACKNOWLEDGEMENTS

The Quapaw Quarter Association is extremely pleased to be the sponsor of **Charles L. Thompson and Associates,** the first critical, book-length treatment of an Arkansas architect and his firm ever published. Though many of the buildings described in this book are in Little Rock, the Association's headquarters, an equal number are in towns and rural hamlets throughout the state. The citizens of DeWitt, Eudora, Fordyce, McGehee, Newport, Tupelo, and dozens of other communities can — and should — be proud that their forefathers commissioned architects such as Thompson to design their most handsome homes and commercial buildings.

The QQA's involvement in this project would not have been possible without the support of many individuals and institutions. Foremost among these has been F. Hampton Roy. Dr. Roy's determined leadership of the project from its inception, together with his very generous financial support, should be a model for those wishing to become enlightened patrons of the arts and humanities. Everyone in Arkansas concerned with the preservation of this state's finest, or most representative, architecture owes him their thanks.

Several private foundations made sizeable grants towards the publication of this book. They were:

Arkansas Community Foundation

Barrett Hamilton Foundation

The Rebsamen Fund

Members and friends of the family of Charles L. Thompson gave important gifts, too. The Association is particularly indebted to Mr. & Mrs. Edwin Cromwell and Mr. John Truemper for their fund-raising efforts. Among those who contributed were:

Charles T. Bellingrath

Mrs. Mary B. Boellner

Mr. & Mrs. E. B. Cromwell, in memory of Mary Watkins Thompson

Henrietta T. Cromwell

James M. Dunaway

Pam Dunaway

Carol Mann Eruren, Myra Thibault Gannaway & Woodson Gannaway in memory of Mary Lillian Jones and George W. Thompson

Gaines N. Houston, in memory of Mildred Thompson Houston

Eugene P. and Gertrude C. Levy

Jane Ross

Charles L. Thompson, Jr.

Mrs. Jane C. Thompson

The QQA would also like to thank the firm of Cromwell, Truemper, Levy, Parker & Woodsmall — the successor to Thompson's architectural practice — for its support of the Association and its involvement in this project. We also appreciate the work of the book's talented designers, Suzanne Kittrell and Becky Witsell, and the efforts of our production managers, August House Publishers. Without any one of these contributors, **Charles L. Thompson and Associates** would not have been possible.

Ralph J. Megna, Executive Director
Quapaw Quarter Association, Inc.
November 1982

7

PREFACE

I became interested in historic architecture in downtown Little Rock in 1973 when I bought the Bechle Apartments on East Ninth Street. I had heard of Charles L. Thompson and was familiar with several buildings he was reputed to have designed. The similarity between the Bechle Apartments and these other structures led me to believe that they were designed by the same person. I called Charles Witsell, Jr., a respected local preservationist and architect, and he secured a detailed set of 1910 drawings of the apartments from the archives of the architectural firm of Cromwell, Truemper, Levy, Parker & Woodsmall. Later, I was also able to obtain copies of the original plans for the Ada Thompson Home on Main Street, and the Cornish House on Arch Street, from the same source. These materials greatly facilitated the restoration of these buildings in accurate fashion and also contributed to documentation necessary to nominate them to the National Register of Historic Places, the federal government's official inventory of properties of architectural or historic importance.

These early efforts impressed upon me the quantity and quality of the archives maintained by the Cromwell firm. I soon learned that the collection of drawings existed primarily through the efforts of Edwin B. Cromwell, the chairman emeritus of the architectural firm originally begun by Charles Thompson in the 1880s. The plans had been indexed according to Thompson's office system and, for many years, were stored in his garage attic. In the late 1940s, Cromwell — Thompson's son-in-law — was given the drawings and asked to care for them. Over the years, they shifted from place to place — including the elevator penthouse of the Hall Building and Cromwell's own garage. During the period from 1950 to 1980, the firm acted as curators and regularly made prints of the drawings available to owners and other architects. In 1981, the entire collection, encompassing over 24,000 sheets, was donated to the Old State House Museum.

In 1979 I met Suzanne Wellington, a landscape architect for the Arkansas Governor's Mansion. She had previously worked as an historic researcher for the Old State House, where she had explored the life and projects of Charles Thompson in preparation for an exhibit of his work. The early exposure to Thompson provided by my restoration efforts and Charles Witsell, combined with Ms. Wellington's enthusiasm for researching the Thompson collection, gave me the original impetus to write this book.

When I sat down to organize my thoughts and interests, I determined that there were three issues I wanted to address. First, the Thompson collection had not been systematically catalogued and there was a pressing need to determine its scope and content. Second, I was eager to determine which of the buildings found in the collection still stood and how they now appeared. Finally, I was interested to learn more about why the Thompson firm had survived nearly one hundred years, through booms and depressions, to be-

9

Fig. 1 The Bechle Apartments spurred Dr. Roy's interest in Charles L. Thompson.

come one of the oldest and largest architectural practices in the nation.

With the cooperation of the Cromwell firm, I set up a survey of the archives. The team assigned to this project found approximately 2,000 sets of plans encompassing the work of not only Charles Thompson, but many of his associates — including partners Fred J. H. Rickon, Theodore M. Sanders, and Frank Ginocchio. With this information, we conducted a statewide search for these structures; unfortunately, we found only a small percentage of the projects represented in the archives. I remain uncertain whether the unlocated buildings were demolished, moved, or simply never built. It is my fervent hope, though, that this book and its catalogue of projects will encourage the identification of additional buildings designed by the firm.

I was assisted by many people in this endeavor. My team of researchers included Nan Thompson Ernst, Sandra Taylor Smith, Wilson Stiles, Robert Wilson, John Barton, and Tim Scott. Ms. Ernst and Ms. Smith, who brought their previous research experience in historic architecture to the project, provided valuable assistance in the survey of the drawings, identification of the buildings, and compilation of other information for the book. Wilson Stiles, an architect and recently the State Historic Preservation Officer, prepared technical materials which placed the work of the Thompson firm in its proper historical perspective. Robert Wilson, with his background in blueprint reproduction, assisted in the documentation of the drawings. Tim Scott aided the field survey.

The majority of this book's outstanding photographs were taken by architectural photographers Greg Hursley, Christopher Lark, and Tom Scott Gordon. Bob Dunn of the Arkansas Historic Preservation Program also provided some excellent photography. Each picture is accordingly acknowledged. I also need to express appreciation for the assistance of the owners of Charles Thompson homes, churches, schools, and commercial buildings who allowed us to photograph their properties.

Edwin Cromwell, his partners, and employees at the Cromwell firm were of substantial aid to the project; I am particularly indebted to Margaret Hatchett, Jim Pfeifer, and Arthur Stern. Lucy Robinson, the director of the Old State House Museum, generously permitted us access to previous research and provided the project with much-needed workspace. Jim Watkins, a former exhibits designer for the museum, was also helpful in the early coordination of the researchers. Joan Williams Baldridge, during her tenure as the State Historic Preservation Officer, helped us with photographs and other documentation, as did the staff of the Quapaw Quarter Association. The association's executive director, Ralph J. Megna, also served as editorial consultant and facilitated moving the manuscript toward publication.

The families of the architects have been extremely helpful in providing biographic information and photographs. Edwin and Henrietta Thompson Cromwell, as well as Charles L. Thompson, Jr., furnished information about Mr. Thompson, Sr. Arthur Sanders, Mimi Dickinson, and Hollis Pruitt made available information about Theodore M. Sanders. Bess Ginocchio provided information about Frank Ginocchio. Tom and Pat Harding supplied information about Thomas S. Harding, Jr. Virginia Burton Russell contributed information about Percy deVerne Burton.

My office staff — Renee Massey, Susan Young, Liz Parker, Nobie Gillespie, Debby Kaucher, Kathy Perry, Nanette Webb, Dotty Harrell, Leslie Sheldon, Denise Lipin, Linda Gerrald, Cathy Hall, and Elizabeth Perry — were of great assistance to the project. I am also deeply indebted to many people and organizations across the state who helped to identify hundreds of Thompson buildings. Listed by county, they include:

Arkansas County:
Mrs. Dorothy J. Cove

Chicot County:
Mrs. Dunlap Hurst
George P. Kelly

Clark County:
Mrs. Juanita Barnett

Fig. 2 The elevator penthouse of the Hall Building once served as the Thompson archives.

Conway County:
Mrs. Wayne Lilley

Craighead County:
Craighead County Historical Society

Cross County:
Cross County Historical Society

Drew County:
Drew County Historical Society

Faulkner County:
Dr. Waddy Moore

Garland County:
Inez Cline

Hempstead County:
Mary Medearis
Harry Shiver

10

Hot Spring County:
Mary Beth Bowman

Independence County:
Clyde McGinnis

Jackson County:
Mrs. Ralph McDonald
Lady Elizabeth Luker

Jefferson County:
Jim Leslie
Arthur Stern

Johnson County:
Mrs. R. Mickel

Lee County:
Ann Brown

Lonoke County:
Mark Anthony
J. W. Lipscomb

Miller County:
Elaine Day
Georgia Dailey

Monroe County:
Jo Claire English

Ouachita County:
Floy Pope
Annie Lea Harrell

Union County:
Annie Laurie Spencer Dickinson

Washington County:
Wendy Marshall

White County:
Mrs. Leister Presley
Ruth Browning

Woodruff County:
Mrs. J. B. Kittrell
Jim Conner

Fig. 3 The Cornish House, a Theodore Sanders project, is now home for Hampton and Nancy Roy.

After reviewing these lengthy acknowledgements, it should become clear how I, a certified ophthalmologist with a busy practice, was able to undertake the research, organization, and production of this book. I have enjoyed the able assistance of many people; without their contributions the project would have been impossible. Indeed, my principal roles have been to advise, coordinate, and encourage the work of a diverse group of talented professionals.

I feel that many residents of, and visitors to, Arkansas are not aware of the remarkable historic architecture in the state. Nor are they familiar with the resources — like the Thompson Collection — which exist to help us learn more about our built heritage. I hope this book, in some small measure, will not only serve to document the life and projects of Charles L. Thompson and his associates, but will also encourage others to explore like I have the rich history and culture of Arkansas.

F. Hampton Roy
Little Rock, Arkansas
September 1982

CHAPTER ONE

ARCHITECTURE IN THE NEW INDUSTRIAL AGE

The final decades of the nineteenth century must have been an extraordinarily exciting time to have worked as an architect or builder in America. A period of conspicuous consumption and reckless exploitation, the Gilded Age was in love with the new energy of the mechanized era. Emerging industries and an expanding population required the rapid construction of unprecedented numbers of buildings. Entirely new structural forms — railroad stations, factories, courthouses, hotels, and storefront commercial buildings among them — were the products of the country's mad rush to abandon its rural heritage and become an urban society.

The industrial age had a radical impact on the way buildings were constructed. Standardized and mass-produced components such as windows, doors, bricks, and decorative woodwork gave birth to mail-order building catalogues. Their utility, in turn, was increased by the creation of a sprawling network of railroads that made possible the speedy delivery of goods thousands of miles from their place of manufacture. Together with machine-cut framing lumber and inexpensive wire nails, these building parts reduced the need to employ skilled craftsmen and dramatically shortened the time needed to erect structures of all types.

As might be expected, the wide availability and declining unit cost of construction materials made it possible to assemble buildings which were increasingly ornate and diverse. Exterior trim and siding of wood, cast stone or clay, and metal became part of an evolving vocabulary of building forms which captured the fancy of America. Using factory-made components for repetitious ornamentation, it was possible to achieve a profusion of detail on structures of modest cost. "High style" in architecture soon achieved equal status with fashion in clothing, as prosperous families and companies sought new ways to demonstrate their affluence.

Contributing to this new fascination with building styles, particularly in domestic architecture, was the widespread distribution and use of so-called "pattern books" or "carpenters guides." One of the earliest and most influential of these books, *The Architecture of Country Houses,*

13

The industrial revolution created the need for new building types and designs. Railroad stations, factories, and storefront commercial buildings offered their designers no precedent to follow, and the architects and builders responded to the challenge with a variety of elaborate forms. Grand hotels, such as the Capital Hotel in Little Rock (opposite page, Fig. 4),were among the new age buildings, too. They often replaced much more modest row-style structures from the first half of the 19th Century, such as those on Markham Street (right, Fig. 5) not far from where the Capital Hotel was later erected.

14

The railroads made the transportation of building materials across the country much easier, quicker, and cheaper. The components — including doors, windows, stairs, ornamental trim, and hardware — for "pattern book" houses such as the Chisum House in Little Rock (left, Fig. 6) were often shipped thousands of miles in boxcars. Such prefabrication had its start in England where manufacturers often advertised the virtues of their products (next page, Fig. 7).

was written by Andrew Jackson Downing in 1850. "A blind partiality for any one style in building," said Downing, "is detrimental to the progress of improvement." Guides such as Downing's remained popular into the early twentieth century. Their illustrations, plans, and cost estimates were a powerful enticement to keep up-to-date with the current styles in East Coast or even European cities.

Against this background of technological advancement and increasing design sophistication, the architectural community found that it needed better training for the responsibilities being thrust upon it. Prior to the Civil War, there were no formal opportunities for a technical education in architecture at an American university. The establishment of such a program of study at the Massachusetts Institute of Technology in 1868 was an important step towards the professionalization of the field. So was the establishment of the American Institute of Architects in 1857. However, through the end of the 1800s, most architects received their artistic training as apprentice draftsmen; engineering was often learned by observing the construction practices of skilled tradesmen, if it was learned at all.

Though the Gilded Age's generation of architects may have lacked formal engineering skills, they confidently designed buildings of exuberant form and unconventional plan. With the designers in the largest cities creating the examples, architects in hundreds of towns across the country were challenged to give their clients the kind of buildings they saw when travelling, or in the pages of the pattern books. Even on America's western frontier, there was a rising appetite for elegance and refinement, and men such as Charles L. Thompson were more than eager to relocate in order to feed it. 🦋

15

Fig. 8 By 1887, Little Rock was a booming city at the crossroads of river and railroad traffic.

16

ARKANSAS RIVER

ARGENTA, ARK.

CHAPTER TWO

THE EARLY PARTNERSHIPS

Though Little Rock was a relatively small town during the fifty years following its establishment in 1821, the community played host to a number of active architects. George Weigart came in the 1830s to supervise the construction of the Old State House, designed by fellow Kentuckian Gideon Shryock.[1] Following Weigart's death in 1834, the town appears to have been without the services of an architect until 1844. In that year, a Mr. R. Larrimore advertised himself as "professionally qualified" to make drawings and superintend the construction of buildings "done in any of the five orders of architecture." In addition to being Little Rock's first resident architect, Larrimore was also a practicing undertaker.[2]

Judging from the lack of advertisements in the *Arkansas Gazette,* there were probably no resident "professional" architects or construction supervisers in Little Rock for roughly a decade after Larrimore's departure in 1848. During the 1860s and 1870s, a number of men reported their occupation as "architect" to the census taker; in most cases, they were probably skilled tradesmen who constructed, as well as designed, their clients' buildings. Conspicuous exceptions were H. C. Green and J. D. Edwards, who advertised extensively in the 1871 City Directory and urged the use of their services with maxims such as "build without plans and repent at leisure" and "measure twice, cut once."[3]

By the 1880s, Little Rock was experiencing a tremendous boom. Its population, which had been set at 12,375 people in 1870, would soar to over 25,000 by 1890,[4] making it one of America's 100 largest municipalities. Indeed, Little Rock was finally shedding its frontier village character and acquiring some of the amenities of a modern city. Public utilities, for example, made their first appearance during this period. The construction of sewage and drainage systems, widespread distribution of piped gas and water, and the arrival of electric lights all took place during the decade. The major streets were paved and, after years of

Fig. 9 Charles L. Thompson came to Little Rock in 1886 because it was the "farthest in the wilderness."

walking in the mud and dust, Little Rock residents were treated to their first brick sidewalks.[5]

In addition to the improvements being made to Little Rock's roads and utilities, the landscape was being changed by the construction of the first "high-style" Victorian public buildings. The circumstances were ripe for architects like Benjamin J. Bartlett, who came to Arkansas in 1885. During his four-year residence in Little Rock, he worked

Fig. 10 Green & Edwards advertised extensively in the 1871 City Directory, the first architects to do so.

on a number of distinguished state-funded projects, including the School for the Blind, the Deaf Mute Institute, and the Insane Asylum. He also supervised the construction of the Christ Episcopal Church.[6]

Bartlett, born in 1835, was a native of New Hampshire. Instead of remaining in the home state of his parents, and his wife's grandparents, he chose to relocate on a regular basis. After leaving his family, and before serving in the Union Army during the Civil War, he lived in Maine and Vermont.[7] Bartlett received his professional training from Gridley Bryant, a well-known Boston architect and, afterwards, moved to Chicago and then Des Moines, exhibiting a penchant for working in frontier areas. His next stop was Little Rock, where he would found what is today one of the oldest architectural firms in the nation.[8]

The new architect was apparently well-received

17

by the citizens of Little Rock. In an article written shortly after his arrival, the *Arkansas Gazette* noted:

> There is a growing demand for architectural beauty in residences, and the rapid growth of the city has attracted a number of architects and builders. Several months ago Mr. B. J. Bartlett located in this city, and created quite a revolution in architecture…he has introduced more modern ideas and methods…his designs show much architectural beauty and prove that he is trained in every particular… it is only reasonable to suppose that he will continue to grow in favor in the future.[9]

Business was good for Bartlett in Arkansas, and his office proved to be a useful training ground for aspiring architects. In the summer of 1885, Bartlett hired as his chief draftsman Max Orlopp, Jr., a graduate of the Naval Academy at Annapolis, Maryland. Orlopp stayed with Bartlett for eleven months, then left to open his own office. Shortly afterward, Orlopp formed a partnership with Casper Keusner, and their new firm was soon awarded the commission to design the Pulaski County Courthouse.[10]

Like a listing in the modern telephone book "yellow pages," it was important for late nineteenth-century businessmen to use the City Directories to promote their businesses. Engaged in active competition with Orlopp and Keusner, Bartlett ran this ad for his services in the 1886 City Directory:

> Benjamin J. Bartlett
> Architect and Superintendent of Buildings
> 215 West Markham
> Little Rock, Arkansas
> Long experience in the profession, and an extensive acquaintance with manufacturers and dealers throughout the country enable me to offer Superior Inducements to those contemplating the erection of new buildings, or the remodeling of old ones, and who desire

Fig. 11 The Arkansas State House was the first building in Little Rock known to have been designed by a professional architect.

Neat and Tasty Architecture and thorough construction at an Economical Rate.

With Orlopp's departure from his firm, Bartlett was in need of another draftsman. He found his man through an advertisement posted in a national lumber journal by Charles L. Thompson of Danville, Illinois.[11] Thompson, who was seventeen years of age when he accepted Bartlett's offer, moved to Little Rock in 1886; the community would be his home for over seventy years.

Thompson had become a draftsman without

the benefit of a formal education. Born in November of 1868, he was the third of James C. and Henrietta Lightner Thompson's seven children.[12] By the time young Charles was fourteen, both his parents had died, and he and the other children moved to Indiana from Illinois, where they were placed in the care of relatives. Thompson, whose first job was selling newspapers when he was nine, quit school to work in a mill in order to help support his younger brothers and sisters.

The teenager worked diligently at his new job. As an extra duty, he assisted an architect whose

The Little Rock School for the Blind (left, Fig. 12) was designed by Benjamin Bartlett who advertised himself (below, Fig. 13) as both an architect and superintendent of buildings. The capital city temporarily grew to 40,000 people in 1880 when former president U.S. Grant visited the town (bottom, Fig. 14). By 1900, the permanent population of Little Rock would reach the same figure.

19

B. J. BARTLETT
Architect
—AND—
SUPERINTENDENT ✛ OF ✛ BUILDINGS

office was above the mill. The designer recognized Thompson's potential and soon put him to work at the drafting table. The young man complemented what he learned at the mill with correspondence courses and incessant reading, a trait which lasted his entire life. Combining these lessons-by-mail with practical experience, Thompson soon became a competent draftsman. His proficiency increased rapidly and, while working for two architects named Hunt, he was put in charge of a construction job. Unfortunately, Thompson's youthful supervision was not well accepted by the older workers, so he was soon

back in the office drawing building plans.

The relegation to the drafting table did not sit well with Thompson, so he decided to seek his fortune elsewhere. His 1886 advertisement for employment brought at least three offers — from New York, New Orleans, and Little Rock. He travelled first to New Orleans and, on his way back to Indiana, stopped in Little Rock. While visiting the capital city, Thompson saw many opportunities to employ his architectural experience. He was later quoted as saying that one reason he chose to settle in Little Rock was because it was "the farthest in the wilderness."[13]

Fig. 15 The Pulaski County Courthouse was designed by a former Bartlett assistant, Max Orlopp, Jr., and his partner, Casper Keusner, in the late 1880s.

20

Thompson's talents were quickly recognized by his new employer. In 1888, Thompson joined Bartlett as an architect and full partner in the firm of Bartlett and Thompson.[14] Their work together typically reflected the tastes of the late nineteenth-century architectural publications, where a mix of several building styles was used to achieve a picturesque overall effect. Bartlett's design for the Blind School in Little Rock was a good example of this variety of Victorian architecture. Another is their plan for the J. H. Thompson home in Helena. This house exhibited the necessary picturesque qualities through its shape, which was distinguished by an asymmetrical massing with a projecting bay, porch spindlework, and a delicate ridge cresting on the roof.

When he was not busy at his practice, Bartlett devoted many hours to the establishment and organization of the Arkansas Society of Engineers, Architects, and Surveyors (ASEAS). Due to the influence of founders J. M. Whitlow, a Fayetteville professor of engineering, and Fred J. H. Rickon, the Little Rock city engineer, the society was primarily interested in engineering issues. Its stated goal was the "professional improvement of its members, encouragement of social intercourse among men of practical science, and the advancement of engineering, architecture, and surveying."[15]

Bartlett's involvement with the ASEAS had begun in 1886 when he contacted engineers, architects, and surveyors throughout Arkansas and solicited their interest and participation in such an organization. The response was favorable, and the first meeting was held in Little Rock during November 1887.

During this meeting, committees were formed to pursue the objectives of the society, and Bartlett was assigned to several of these. A number of papers were read, too, including "Municipal Engineer" by Fred Rickon, who was elected the first president of the society, and

Fig. 16 The J. H. Thompson home in Helena is one of the earliest drawings remaining from the partnership of Bartlett and Thompson (c.1888). Its Queen Anne design was typical of the late Victorian period.

"Sanitation" by Bartlett.[16] The latter presentation called attention to the urgent need for adequate sanitary systems and suggested that architects play an important role in determining methods of waste disposal and be knowledgeable in the area. Bartlett was one of the first men in the state to address the growing problem of storm- and wastewater disposal.

The newly formed ASEAS moved quickly to establish a library for its members. Yearly transactions of the society were published in a pamphlet which was distributed to members. The pamphlet also served as an exchange for publications from similar organizations throughout the country. The publication included the society's business and minutes, papers delivered at the meetings, and a classified section. In the first edition, Bartlett took out this advertisement:

Benjamin J. Bartlett
Architect and Superintendent of Buildings
Odd Fellows Block, Little Rock
Specialities: Public Buildings and Churches

Through the society, Thompson was brought into contact with others in the building trades, and his organizational and leadership skills became evident. For the second meeting of the ASEAS, held in Little Rock in November 1888, Thompson "designed and executed...a very elaborate blueprint" as the title page for the meeting program.[17] Also during the meeting, he was officially recognized as a peer by his older and more experienced fellows in his election to the architect's grade of membership and was asked to serve on the Standing Committee on Architecture.[18]

In 1890, Bartlett learned that a new courthouse building was being planned for a delta county in Mississippi. Anxious to move on but encumbered with unfinished work and unpaid financial obligations, Bartlett proposed that Thompson complete the work undertaken by the firm and assume the liabilities in exchange for the assets. The deal was struck, and Bartlett moved on to Mississippi.[19]

Thompson, who had married Lillian McGann in July 1889, carried on the firm's operations at the same location under the name "Charles L. Thompson, Architect and Superintendent." To be both husband and business owner was a tremendous task for so young a man. He was often asked why Mr. Thompson had "sent his son, instead of coming himself" to inspect the construction of buildings he had designed.[20] Thompson's demonstrated ability, however, and his excellent standing with other professionals through his association with the ASEAS enabled him to conduct his business respectably and with aplomb.

By remaining in Little Rock, Thompson distinguished himself from the common practices of other architects of the period. Frequently, designers and superintendents would be attracted to a community by word of a pending construction project. Since the project was their only real tie to the community, there was no commitment to remain beyond its completion. Upon learning of another project elsewhere, they would simply pull up stakes and leave. As a result, many had the reputation of transients, with all the personal habits which accompanied the title. Few of these architects were concerned with, or adept in, business management, and it was not unusual for them to be behind in their financial obligations.[21] Thompson, however, established an aura of permanence and strong community commitment. His sense of civic responsibility, combined with his business acumen, greatly contributed to his success.

Thompson's practice was further enhanced by his participation in social and civic organizations. He joined the Western Star Masonic Lodge No. 2 soon after coming to Little Rock and became a Master Mason in 1889; he was elected master of his lodge in 1894. Thompson was also a member of the Knight's Templar.[22] Through these organizations, the young architect remained in contact with business and community leaders

22

CHAS. L. THOMPSON,
Architect and Superintendent
ODD FELLOWS BUILDING, LITTLE ROCK, ARK.

Fig. 17 After Bartlett's departure, Thompson had a one-man practice. His advertisement in the 1890 City Directory suggests his interest in the then-popular Stick and Shingle styles of architecture.

Fig. 18 With F.J.H. Rickon, Thompson entered and won a design competition for the monumental Little Rock Exposition Hall. Though the building was never constructed, Rickon and Thompson became partners in 1891.

Fig. 19 The Judge W. E. Hemingway House in Little Rock was a Rickon & Thompson design in the elaborate Queen Anne style.

in Little Rock and elsewhere in Arkansas. They demonstrated their confidence in Thompson by awarding him commissions to design their residences and places of business.

In 1890, a group of Little Rock businessmen assembled to make plans for a major exhibition and state fair which would showcase the progress Arkansas had made in the late nineteenth century. The building committee for the Little Rock Exposition, in an effort to obtain the best plans possible, solicited proposals for the main exhibit hall from architectural firms throughout the state. For this competition, Thompson joined forces with Fred J. H. Rickon, the Canadian-born city engineer and past president of the ASEAS. While the proposal submitted by Rickon and Thompson was approved, and they were paid for their work, the building was never constructed. Years later Thompson was heard to say the exhibition hall was "just a dream."[23]

Although the dream was never realized, the two professionals profited from the publicity and learned they could work well together. They soon officially combined their talents by creating the firm of Rickon & Thompson, Architects and Civil Engineers, on January 15, 1891, and established offices in the Allis Building across the street from the Old State House.[24] This partnership had special historical significance, for it represented one of the earliest professional associations of an architect and an engineer within a single firm. The combination of skills made it possible to approach projects which other design firms at the time would have found difficult to execute.

The buildings designed by Thompson during his association with Rickon were, by and large, in keeping with the styles and fashions of the works by his contemporaries. Nearly all architects of the period relied upon publications which provided designs, details, and specifications for structures in an interminable listing of styles. It was left to men such as Thompson to make, in consultation

23

Fig. 20 The William Ragland House, a near twin of the Hemingway House (page 23), was constructed in 1895. Its shingled exterior accounts for the shimmering shadows on the second floor.

24

The Rector Bath House in Hot Springs (below, Fig. 21) was a Romanesque style structure which resembled the buildings of the great 19th century architect, H. H. Richardson. The fanciful interior of the M. M. Cohn home in Little Rock (right, Fig. 22) exemplified the Victorian philosophy that "too much was not enough."

with their clients, their own interpretation, predicated upon the available materials, budget, and local trade skills.

When the firm of Rickon & Thompson was established in 1891, the "Queen Anne" style was near the height of its popularity. It had first caught the American public's eye in 1876 at the Centennial Exhibition in Philadelphia, where three buildings in that mode were presented by Great Britain. Two years later, the author and architect Henry Hudson Holly wrote, "The Queen Anne Revival shows the influence of Francis I, which is now indeed to be arranged under the general head of free classic, but it is also influenced by what is known as 'cottage architecture' of that period." The Queen Anne style in the United States, however, evolved into something which was uniquely American. Enthusiastically employing such tools of the Machine Age as jigsaws, bandsaws, and lathes, the Yankees fashioned a kind of "architecture as art" which was replete with a level of ornamentation previously unknown to American buildings. Even though architects and builders invented many different stylistic interpretations, they were all consistent with the Victorian demands for picturesque outline and variety of texture, all achieved through the combination of decorative treatments.

The Rickon & Thompson design for the Hemingway House in Little Rock shows the strong influence of the Queen Anne fashion, while the Ragland House, also in the capital city, illustrates that style at its highest and most elaborate. In Hot Springs, their design for the Rector Bath House exemplifies the asymmetry and fanciful geometry of Queen Anne architecture, with a hint of the Romanesque style in the brick arches. Thompson's facade for the Home Insurance Company in Fordyce also features some Romanesque details in the squat columns and stone voussoirs, combined with the picturesque corner turret and classic pilasters. The whole structure is a good example of commercial Victorian architecture that conveys feelings of security and solidarity, as well as stylishness. These were, of course, prerequisites for a landmark structure in a new and growing small town in Arkansas.

An 1895 New Year's greeting book published by Rickon & Thompson lists nearly fifty projects either completed or underway. While the vast majority are residential commissions (including one for prominent Arkansas politician Jeff Davis), the portfolio also catalogues several college and school buildings, two banks, a dozen commercial structures, a hotel, and a courthouse. The holiday salutation on the first inside page, though, makes it clear that the firm's bread-and-butter came from

26

Fig. 23 The Temple B'nai Israel in Little Rock was an 1897 Rickon & Thompson project. It stood on the site now occupied by the First National Bank Building.

The Home Insurance Company Building in Fordyce (below, Fig. 24) was constructed in 1906 and was similar to the Bank of Fordyce (below right, Fig. 25), also on Main Street, but designed c.1890.

single-family homes, not the business projects:

> *To those who happy homes have always known,*
> *To those who plan and work, such homes to own,*
> *To all who building homes would bless mankind,*
> *To all who in their homes a refuge find.* [25]

Thompson and Rickon worked together for six years before dissolving their partnership in April of 1897.[26] While Rickon pursued other business interests as the vice-president of the Mechanics Building and Loan Association, Thompson continued the work of his architectural firm. For the next two decades, Thompson — with the help of a changing coterie of assistants — solidified his claim to be the leading architect in the state. Though he changed the landscape of Arkansas with distinctive homes and commercial structures in a style uniquely his own, his masterwork was the solid establishment of an "architectural association" which would grow and prosper for decades past his active practice. 🌀

27

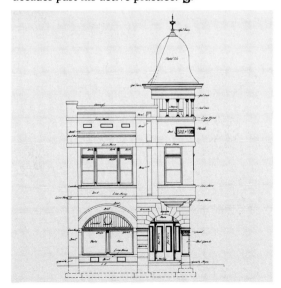

Fig. 26 Charles Thompson designed the C. A. Wooten House in Helena for its dramatic, elevated site in 1915.

CHAPTER THREE

CHARLES L. THOMPSON, ARCHITECT

The years from 1897 to 1916 were the most productive of Charles Thompson's long professional career. Combining a keen business mind with creative architectural skills, he secured design commissions for hundreds of projects ranging from modest cottages to large commercial and governmental buildings. His reputation, in part built upon the unique qualities of his work as well as its sheer quantity, spread throughout Arkansas and into neighboring states.

Though he had no formal partners during this period, Thompson was assisted by a number of employees who contributed to the success of the firm. One of the first to join him was Thomas Harding, Jr. The son of a respected Little Rock architect with whom Thompson had become well acquainted, Harding was hired in 1898 at the age of fourteen.[1] The youngster had a natural talent for the profession and soon became an excellent draftsman. Like Thompson himself, Harding acquired most of his architectural education through experience, reading, and correspondence courses. As his proficiency increased, Harding was given more responsibility for Thompson's residential projects and, in 1916, became a partner in the firm.

Another invaluable assistant was Percy deVerne Burton, who was hired as a draftsman in 1908 to work with Thomas Harding. Burton was from Winchester, Virginia and had moved to Little Rock from St. Louis in 1904.[2] Before joining Thompson's firm, Burton served in the army and had operated his own architectural office for one year.[3] Burton, whose drawings were characterized by fluidity and grace, was a draftsman of extraordinary skill. He was a faithful employee of the firm for over fifty years.

Thompson was an outstanding role model for his young apprentices. He was meticulous and disciplined in his work and spent many evenings at home in study. He had access to the ASEAS library, and had a large and diverse personal collection of books.[4] Thompson kept abreast of developments in his field by subscribing to several architectural journals and by occasionally travelling to see the work of other designers. He also had a broad knowledge of history, philosophy, and literature, and was "thoroughly conversant in leading topics of the day."[5]

Despite Thompson's lack of academic training in architecture, his extensive reading ensured that he remained sensitive to the changes taking place in his profession at the end of the nineteenth century. After forty years of infatuation with picturesque eclecticism, America's leading designers had begun looking for new and simpler shapes for their buildings. Their search, generally speaking, took them in three divergent directions.

One was the "Craftsman" style, named for the popular architectural magazine of the same title published by designer Gustav Stickley. Craftsman buildings made extensive use of natural materials such as stone, large caliber timbers, textured stucco, and clay tile. This style, principally used for homes, declined in popularity after the magazine ceased publication in 1916.

In opposition to this newest revival of the quaint, English cottage style, avant-garde Ameri-

Thomas Harding, Sr., was a distinguished architect whose son went to work for Thompson after his death. His home (below left, Fig. 27) was located on Broadway in Little Rock. The Craftsman Magazine *(below right, Fig. 28) influenced architecture nationwide at the turn of the century.*

VOL. XIV, NO. 6   SEPTEMBER, 1908   25 CENTS

THE CRAFTSMAN

REVIVAL OF SPANISH ART AT THE SALON
POSTAL SAVINGS BANKS AND PARCEL POST
IMPORTANCE OF THE SCHOOL NURSE'S WORK
PHYSICAL CULTURE FOR BLIND CHILDREN

TWENTY-NINE-WEST-THIRTY-FOURTH-STREET-NEW-YORK

29

can architects began exploring Modernism and
Classicism. The former found its leading expo-
nents in men like Louis Sullivan and Frank
Lloyd Wright who experimented with new
building shapes made possible by the innova-
tive use of steel beams and reinforced concrete.
Classicism, on the other hand, signalled the re-
birth of eighteenth-century American Georgian,
Federal, and Adamesque styles. The deliberate
stylistic employment of forms associated with
ancient Greek democracy and Roman justice
ensured its popularity after the successful use of
these classical themes at the World's Columbian
Exposition of 1893 in Chicago.

Thompson could not help but be influenced by
the interest of his clients in classical architecture.
Many of his first designs in the Colonial Revival
style were transitional, though, since they employed eighteenth-century details on what was
basically a Queen Anne building. His plans for
the Ferrell House in Batesville were typical of
many other projects: A Queen Anne house, with
its asymmetrical massing and Victorian turret,
was cosmetically treated to a classical porch and
balustrade, a Palladian window in the gable, and
a classical frieze.

*The J. W. Ferrell House in Batesville (below and
right, figs. 29 & 30) exhibits both Queen Anne and
Colonial Revival features.*

30

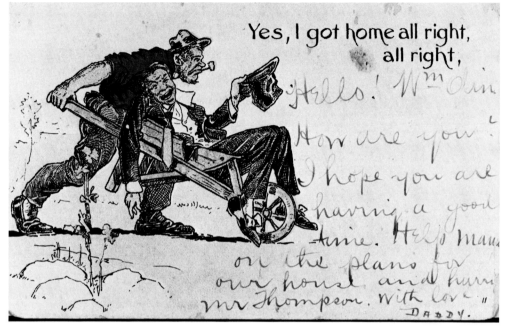

Though little of Thompson's professional correspondence remains, it appears that he enjoyed the esteem of his many clients. For example, Mr. E. S. Ready of Helena wrote the architect on August 20, 1910:

> After having occupied our new house for several weeks both Mrs. Ready and I feel that in justice to you we must tell you how delighted we are with the home that you planned and superintended.
>
> While you have planned very many houses handsomer and more expensive than ours, I do not believe that you have ever designed one that looks more home-like and is generally admired than our Jacobean residence. As an exemplification of this, there is another house nearing completion in Helena that will cost probably three times as much as ours, and yet I believe that 90% of the people who have seen them both prefer our home.
>
> You have made it possible for us to own and occupy a place of abode in which we take great pride, and in addition thereto your work, and that of your assistants all thru have been such as to make dealing with you a genuine pleasure.

Of course, not everyone was quite so flowery in their praise. In 1908, Mr. W. O. Hardeman wrote to his son in regard to a new home they were building on State Street in Little Rock: "Help Mama on the plans for our house and hurry Mr. Thompson."

Thompson's transitional cottages were particularly interesting, since they were — in many cases — creative variations on the same theme. He used a common floor plan and exterior massing, and then varied the scale, roof line, and ornamentation to suit the client. In his designs for three attractive Little Rock cottages, he simply alternated between hipped and gabled dormers, Palladian windows and fanlights, and Ionic and Tuscan architectural orders to give the buildings individuality. Even in his commercial structures, such as his plans for a store for R. E. Robertson of Jonesboro, Thompson frequently recycled an earlier design. The Robertson building had a very Victorian storefront, yet a fashionable Palladian window gave it the requisite stamp of Classicism.

In addition to new designs that resulted in eclectic buildings, Thompson received a number of commissions to design stylish classical renovation treatments for aging Victorians. Colonel J. E. Little of Conway believed a simple one-story porch with Ionic columns could bring his house up-to-date. Interior walls in the Carpenter Gothic home of Robert Johnson were replaced with fluted Corinthian columns to create larger living areas; a plan to give this Little Rock house a classically inspired porch was never carried out. For those clients with deeper pocketbooks and more sweeping aspirations, the architect could design a complete remodelling. Thompson presented Walter W. Brown of Camden with two alternatives to make his residence as classically palatial as possible.

Thompson designed many Colonial Revival cottages in the early 20th Century. The A. J. Wilson (below, Fig. 31) and J. D. Back Houses (right, Fig. 32), both in Little Rock, show how porches and windows could be varied to produce different houses on similar floor plans.

THE FRONT ELEVATION

Fig. 33 The W. R. Stewart House in the Centennial Addition of Little Rock was designed in 1910. Its formal porch wraps around an asymmetrical structure reminiscent of the late Victorian period.

Fig. 34 The three Colonel B. S. Johnson homes are modified Colonial Revival "boxes" which alternate the use of gable bays and dormers to create variety in their appearance. The porches also exhibit subtle differences.

34

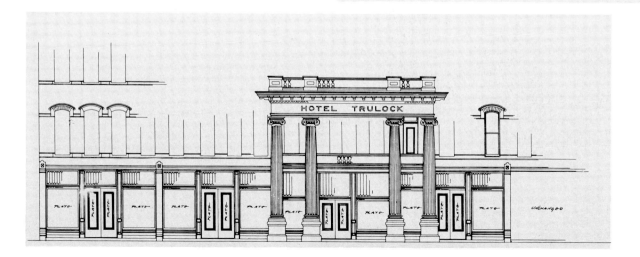

*Alterations were an important part of Thompson's
architectural practice at the turn-of-the-century. The
J. E. Little House in Conway (right, Fig. 35) was
treated to a classically inspired porch in 1911. The
Hotel Trulock in Pine Bluff (below, Fig. 36) was remodelled a decade earlier with a portico similar to
the one Thompson used on one of its better-known
contemporaries, the Terminal Hotel, in Little Rock.*

When remodelling Walter W. Brown's home in Camden, Thompson presented his client with two alternative ways of making his home more impressive. One (above left, Fig. 37) involved a monumental two-story portico and the other (above right, Fig. 38) a balustraded porch with roof dormers. In a new commercial building for R. E. Robertson in Jonesboro (right, Fig. 39), Thompson added a central Palladian window — an avant-garde touch for a structure designed in 1899.

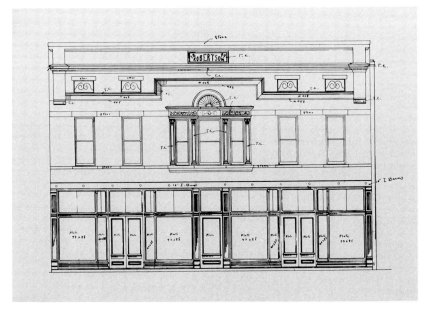

Fig. 40 The Walter Nash House in Little Rock combines a monumental, two-story portico and Colonial Revival details with a Victorian-like floor plan. Designed in 1907 as a single-family residence, it has since been converted to professional offices.

Eventually, Thompson began discarding Victorian qualities from his designs and produced buildings of traditional classical character. The Walter Nash House, built in Little Rock in 1904, combined pure Colonial Revival details with one of Thompson's last asymmetrical floor plans. The J. W. Pugh home in Portland was typical of his later designs; it was basically a two-story box, capped with a hipped roof and wide eaves, and surrounded by a one-story classical porch. Thompson's own home employed the same classical box, but also featured such eclectic details as squat columns, tile roof, and a Dutch gable dormer. He also made temple-front buildings with pedimented porticos popular in Arkansas. The J. C. Marshall House in Little Rock, as well as the public library in Arkadelphia, were well-executed examples of that style.

Though the firm employed the Colonial Revival style chiefly for residences, it was sensitive to the other types of Classicism which were made immensely popular at the Chicago Exposition in 1893. In Thompson's design for Little Rock City Hall, and in the Thompson and Harding plan for a mausoleum at Mt. Holly Cemetery, he demonstrated an affinity for austere Neoclassicism. The mausoleum is quite Greek in its heaviness and simplicity; on the other hand, the city hall is more Roman in its delicacy and Pantheon-like dome.

Occasionally, Thompson indulged in the revival of historical styles completely divorced from Classicism. His finest and most academically accurate design in Gothic form is his plan for St. Edward's Catholic Church in Little Rock. Even more unique was the home he designed for John R. Fordyce in the Egyptian mode. This 1904 structure was complete with pylon facade and papyrus capitals.

37

38

Front Elevation I

The J. W. Pugh House in Portland (left, Fig. 41) was designed in 1916 and is typical of many of the homes for which Thompson prepared plans before World War I. Its boxy shape is capped by a modified hip roof and dormer windows, while the single-story porch is supported by classically inspired columns. The exposed rafters were a characteristic of Craftsman architecture which Thompson was fond of employing on what were otherwise Colonial Revival buildings. His own home in Little Rock (right, Fig. 42) was a classic box form ornamented with a tile roof and Mission-style dormer.

Fig. 43 When the J. C. Marshall House in Little Rock was constructed in 1908 the street on which it was located — South Arch — was the chief route out of the city towards Benton. The use of a Greek temple-like facade permitted Thompson to endow the home with an impressive stature despite its modest, two-story scale.

40

Almost Spartan in appearance, this mausoleum at Mt. Holly Cemetery in Little Rock (right, Fig. 44) relied on its symmetrical design, classical details, and honest use of materials to convey a sense of quiet dignity. The Public Library at Arkadelphia (left, Fig. 45) made use of the same features in a far more elaborate fashion.

City Hall, Little Rock, Arkansas

Fig. 46 Little Rock City Hall was one of the capital city's most impressive public buildings when it was constructed in 1907. Its central dome, arched windows, and monumental portico were important elements in the sense of Roman grandeur necessary to early 20th Century government buildings.

Fig. 47 The John R. Fordyce House was the most unique building ever designed by Thompson. Constructed in 1904, the Egyptian Revival residence featured sloping exterior walls, pylons with papyrus capitals, and a wide roof overhang. Inside, the house boasted embossed metallic wallpaper and extensive wood panelling.

42

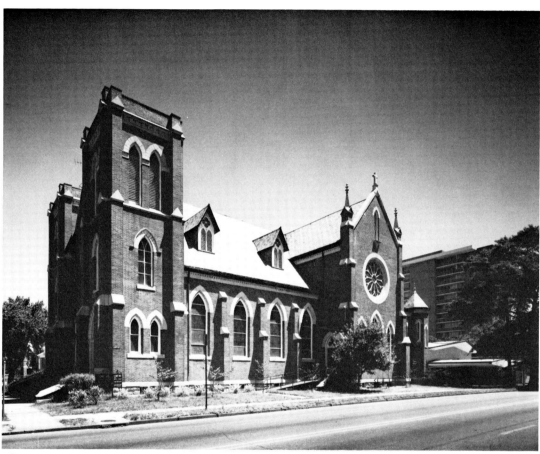

43

FRONT ELEVATION

"Tower to be Built to Ht. indicated By Dotted line" were the notations Charles Thompson made on his drawing for the front elevation of the St. Edwards Catholic Church (left, Fig. 48) in Little Rock. The steeples, as instructed, were never constructed (above, Fig. 49), although the building does feature outstanding Gothic detailing and a beautifully patterned slate roof.

At the same time that his professional fortunes were rapidly rising, a personal tragedy sadly complicated Thompson's private life. His wife, Lillian, contracted tuberculosis and was compelled to make numerous trips to Arizona in the hope that the climate would restore her health. All the efforts, however, were futile, and Thompson's dear "Lillie" died in 1904. Her passing left Thompson, still only thirty-six, with two young daughters and a son. He called upon his sister, then living in Wisconsin, to come to Little Rock and care for his family.[6]

Thompson then threw himself into his work; indeed, many of his most outstanding structures were designed during this period in his life. Perhaps his masterpiece was the immense Colonial Revival residence for Peter Hotze, a highly successful Little Rock cotton broker. This baronial brick house was distinguished by a monumental semi-circular portico supported by two pairs of fluted columns. Apparently Thompson's reputation commanded a great deal of respect, for despite Hotze's use of the local architect, he reportedly employed Tiffany Studios of New York to fashion the interior.[7]

Thompson designed many grand residences for those who were financially able to indulge in the latest architectural fashion. The home of the Honorable E. H. Conner in Augusta is one of many "mansions" he designed. Sometimes, four or six colossal columns did not make enough of a "statement," so Thompson provided a one-story classical porch which extended around the front three sides of the house, which was set back behind a monumental two-story portico. Such was also the case for the W. S. McClintock House in Marianna. Another unusual treatment, employed on a home for A. N. Tanner of Helena, consisted of a classical pediment projecting from a huge gambrel roof that was supported by large Corinthian columns.

Fig. 50 The "new" Peter Hotze House, constructed at the turn of the century, was probably the most architecturally significant single-family home designed by Charles L. Thompson and led to a series of commissions for monumental residences. This Little Rock structure is located immediately adjacent to the woodframe Italianate cottage which Hotze built for his family after the Civil War.

FRONT ELEVATION.
SHEET NO.1

Both the E. H. Conner House in Augusta (left, Fig. 51) and the W. S. McClintock House in Marianna (above, Fig. 52) are extraordinary examples of Thompson's skill for designing large, impressive homes in the Colonial Revival style. In many small towns across Arkansas, residences such as these have become local social — as well as architectural — landmarks.

Fig. 53 Sited amid a grove of century-old trees and next to Bearskin Lake, Marlsgate — the plantation home of the Dortch family at Scott — has been little altered since its construction in 1904. To support the two-story portico, Thompson designed unusual square brick columns with cast Ionic capitals.

46

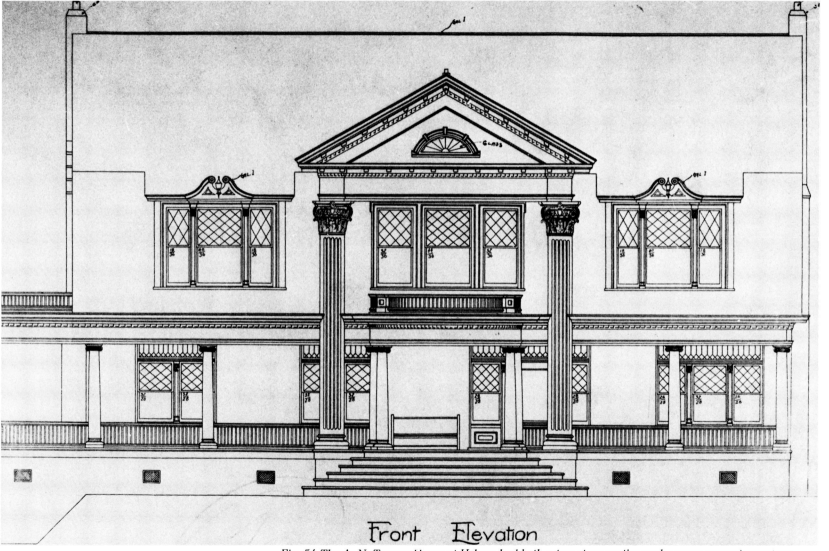

Front Elevation

Fig. 54 The A. N. Tanner House at Helena had both a two-story portico and a wrap-around one-story veranda. The design was also unique for its employment of a gambrel — barn-shaped — roof with projecting ornamented dormers.

In addition to designing an extraordinary number of important residences, Charles Thompson's firm played a leading role in establishing the standards for courthouse architecture in Arkansas. Fifteen county courthouses, including the outstanding 1905 Washington County Courthouse, were designed by his office. These structures, along with Thompson's city halls and numerous schools, had a profound effect on the appearance of public buildings throughout the state for several decades.

48

A number of small changes were made in the design of the Washington County Courthouse (above, Fig. 55 and right, Fig. 56) when it was constructed in 1905. The most significant alteration of the plan was the removal of the belvedere from above the clock in the tower.

Thompson's county courthouses set the standards for public buildings all over Arkansas in the early 20th Century. The modest Cleveland County Courthouse in Rison (left, Fig. 57) and the more ambitious Monroe County Courthouse in Clarendon (right, Fig. 58) illustrate the architect's fondness of buff brick, clock towers, and symmetrical appearances.

Fig. 59 The F. N. Croxon House in Little Rock.

50

Thompson's most significant contribution as a designer, however, was his firm's development of a peculiar synthesis of styles for residences built after 1910. Thompson and his assistants were unquestionably influenced by both the work of Frank Lloyd Wright and Gustav Stickley. The organic spatial flow, wide overhanging eaves, shallow roof pitches, simplicity of ornamentation, and low proportions of Wright's "Prairie" style houses were easily melded with the designs promoted by Stickley's *Craftsman Magazine*. In turn, these twentieth-century styles could be combined with Thompson's favored Colonial Revival mode to create homes unique to the Mid-South.

The residence of Forrest N. Croxon in Little Rock, for example, featured a traditional Colonial form of the gambrel roof extending over the main body of the house and supported by Craftsman brackets. The home's columns were somewhat Tuscan, yet also Craftsman in their heavy proportions. Another extraordinary example of Thompson's mixed styles was the Charles Walls home in Lonoke. Its portico and entry doors are classical, but its linear massing, windows, wide eaves, and exposed rafters are more typical of Prairie and Craftsman architecture.

Occasionally the Thompson firm abandoned classical influences altogether. Its horizontal lines, intimacy with the natural surroundings, and lack of any historic design allusions made the J. Hicks Deener House in Searcy one of Thompson's most Craftsman-like homes. The same qualities appeared in many of the cottages and bungalows the firm designed immediately prior to World War I. At the same time, residences for Shelby England and Alex Keith, as well as the Al Amin Temple, all in Little Rock, demonstrate Thompson's willingness to experiment with designs which nearly approached the Prairie ideal.

(text continues on page 64)

Fig. 60 The Al Amin Temple in Little Rock is one of Arkansas's best Prairie School buildings. This style, made popular by architect Frank Lloyd Wright, is characterized by horizontal banding, a central block with lower flanking extentions, narrow casement windows, and projecting eaves.

52

The Thompson firm became quite adept at designing Craftsman style buildings for a variety of different uses. The W. E. Collier House in Pine Bluff (left, Fig. 61) harmoniously blends stone, stucco, wood, and glazed tile to create a modest, but very attractive residence. Thompson's plan for C. A. F. Smith's apartment house in Little Rock (above, Fig. 62) used similar materials but with completely different results. The W. E. Hemingway barn in Fayetteville (next page, Fig. 63) demonstrates that Charles Thompson could interpret the Craftsman style for even utilitarian buildings.

54

The Craftsman style could, in Thompson's hands, be stretched to cover an amazing range of building sites. The J. Hicks Deener bungalow in Searcy (left, Fig. 64) and the Dr. F. O. Rogers House in Little Rock (right, Fig. 65) share common features — including wide eaves with exposed rafter ends and gable-roofed dormers — despite their disparity in scale.

The step from Craftsman to the Prairie School often was not far. The A. M. Keith House in Little Rock (left, Fig. 66) combined features of both styles, while a few blocks away the Shelby England House (below right, Fig. 67) more closely conforms to the expectations of the Prairie School of architecture.

55

Fig. 68 D. Ward Dunlap House in Clarksville, 1906.

Fig. 69 W. K. Ramsey House in Camden, 1904.

*Thompson and his associates made alterations to buildings which could be dramatic or subtle.
The Victorian Charles Vestal House in Little Rock (left, Fig. 70) and M. A. Austin House in Pine Bluff
(right, Fig. 71) were remodelled in 1900 with the addition of stylish Colonial Revival porches. The Charles
Walls House in Lonoke (next page, Fig. 72) was designed by Thompson in 1912 and sensitively enlarged by
his successor office, the Cromwell firm, half a century later.*

58

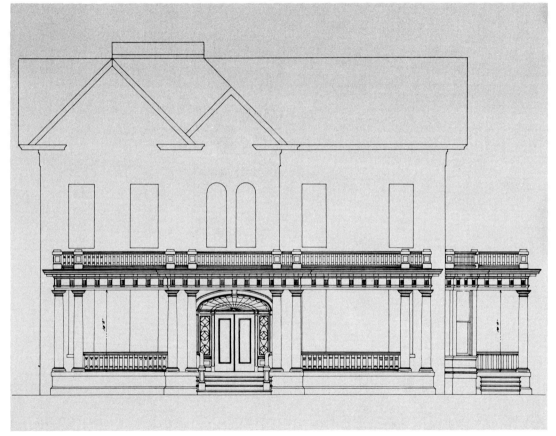

60

Institutional and commercial architecture was an important part of the design business for the Thompson firm. The presence throughout Arkansas of edifices such as the Clark County Courthouse in Arkadelphia (Fig. 73), constructed in 1899, greatly enhanced Thompson's reputation and helped seal contracts to plan many private homes and buildings.

61

The Hospital & Benevolent Association in Pine Bluff
commissioned Thompson to design the Davis Hospital Building
(left, Fig. 74) in 1908. His restrained treatment of that structure
contrasts with the elaborate facade he proposed for the Prescott
Hotel (above, Fig. 75) in Prescott, Arkansas.

Churches and school facilities, though not as important to his firm's practice before World War I as afterwards, are well represented in Thompson's 1897-1916 portfolio. The First Baptist Church in Conway (opposite page, Fig. 76) is a handsome 1909 building with a distinctive central dome roofed in barrel tile. The St. Mark's Church in Hope (above, Fig. 77) is a modest frame vernacular sanctuary with delicate stained-glasswork. The 1900 University of Arkansas dormitory at Fayetteville (right, Fig. 78) combines Craftsman and Colonial Revival features.

In 1908, four years after the death of his
first wife, Thompson married Mary Watkins, the
daughter of a prominent and long established family in Arkansas.[8] The return of a normal home life
for Thompson appears to have been a major factor
in his increasing involvement in activities outside the office. Just a year later, for example, he
accepted an appointment by newly elected Governor George Donaghey to head a commission
which would oversee the completion of the state
capitol building. This appointment was the first
of Thompson's long and prestigious contributions
to public projects in Arkansas.

Below left, Fig. 79 Charles L. Thompson was a prospering architect who was mature before his years when, in 1909, Governor George Donaghey appointed him to chair the commission to oversee the completion of the Arkansas State Capitol (below right, Fig. 80).

64

Below, Fig. 81 Governor George Donaghey. Thompson's long-time assistant, and later partner, Thomas Harding, Jr., had an avid interest in the fire fighting service. He is pictured here (below left, Fig. 82) in front of the Thompson-designed Central Fire Station.

65

Controversy had surrounded the construction of the capitol since its beginning in 1899. Governor Donaghey had based much of his campaign on a pledge to complete the building. His idea of a committee of professionals, whose advice would enable him to expedite construction work, was formalized with Thompson's appointment as chairman. With the aid of the committee, the project made great progress; the original contractor was replaced, and plans were quickly assembled to reconstruct those portions of the building found to be inadequate. In 1911, the legislature and some state administrative offices were able to move to the building; the rest of the capitol was completed in 1915. Afterwards, Governor Donaghey said of his choice for commission chairman, "Mr. Thompson was known to be a man of high character, a good architect, and an excellent businessman."[9]

As Thompson began to become more involved in civic affairs, he turned more and more of the responsibility for the architectural office over to Thomas Harding. The younger man's work was highly regarded, too, and he was occasionally called upon to take projects independent of the firm. In 1915, Harding drew the plans for the Pulaski Heights Fire Station.[10] This opportunity marked a major advancement in his career, for until then, he had worked primarily on residential commissions.

With the completion of the design for the fire station, Thompson's confidence in Harding's ability increased. In the following year, the assistant was offered a partnership with Thompson; with his acceptance, the firm was renamed Thompson & Harding, Architects.[11] Thompson, who was eager to use his reputation to attract large projects such as commercial structures, schools, and public buildings, was pleased to have a capable partner with whom to share the responsibility of the firm.

The beginning of Thompson & Harding, Architects, in 1916 signalled the end of an era for Thompson. Even though the firm's best employees had exercised considerable authority for many years, the overriding design and management direction had been coming from Thompson himself. Internal changes brought about by the new partnership, along with Thompson's growing interest in outside activities, would soon combine to alter the dynamics of the firm and the complexion of Arkansas architecture. 🦡

Fig. 83 The Little Rock YMCA Building, later the offices for the Arkansas Democrat, *was designed and built in 1904 by Charles Thompson. Two years later, George R. Mann designed the classically inspired commercial structure at its right.*

CHAPTER FOUR

COLLEAGUES AND COMPETITORS

Charles L. Thompson was easily the most prolific Arkansas architect of his age and, by virtue of the sheer number and quality of his projects, perhaps the most important. There were, however, other distinguished architects practicing in Little Rock at that time, and several of them were easily Thompson's equals as designers. Though none of his peers ever had the kind of pervasive impact on the appearance of Arkansas's single-family residences that Thompson did, they left a considerable legacy in the form of commercial and public architecture throughout the state.

The most renowned of Thompson's Arkansas contemporaries was George R. Mann. Originally from Indiana, Mann was a thoroughly trained and experienced architect in his mid-forties when he came to Little Rock in 1900 to design and build the new state capitol. Like so many designers of his age, he had received his early training as an apprentice draftsman. After two years at the drawing table, his employer urged him to attend the fledgling architecture program at the Massachusetts Institute of Technology. From there, he worked for a brief time in the famed New York architectural firm of McKim, Meade and White. At the age of twenty-one he moved west and began designing on his own or in short-lived partnerships with other architects.[1]

Early in his career, Mann established himself as an adept designer of large business and government buildings. Before moving to Little Rock, he had received commissions for a post office, city hall, theater, hotel, railroad station, and many office and mercantile structures. He had also entered competitions to design state capitols in Washington, Minnesota, and Montana. He won the competition in Montana, but the building was never constructed according to his original plans, due to the state's inability to finance the project.[2]

After moving to Little Rock and beginning work on the Arkansas State Capitol, Mann was asked to design a number of important local buildings. Among the projects he completed were the Marion Hotel, the Arkansas Gazette Building, the "new" addition to the Pulaski County Courthouse, the State Bank (Boyle) Building, and the Gus Blass (Fabco) Building. In 1913 he formed a partnership with Austrian Eugene J. Stern and was responsible for the design of such Arkansas landmarks as the Arlington Hotel in Hot Springs and the Masonic Temple in Little Rock.[3]

Mann was a noted practitioner of "high-style" neoclassical architecture. Many of his buildings exemplified the Beaux Arts School's attention to elaborate detail, particularly at the roofline and around entranceways. As a rule, too, Mann's projects adhered to a strict classical sense of proportion, massing, and symmetry. For building materials, Mann nearly always used masonry or stone, and frequently employed terra-cotta tile for decoration. Through this careful choice of exterior fabrics and design, he could make modestly scaled buildings — like his own offices on East Capitol in Little Rock — appear monumental.

Another Arkansas builder with a penchant for classical architecture was Frank Gibb. He was the son of a well-to-do Chicago family whose business was destroyed by the fire of 1871. While Gibb apparently had experience as a surveyor and engineer, little is known of his training as a building designer. By 1903, though, he was representing himself as an architect.[4] Among the classically inspired structures he is known to have designed were his own home, a peculiar building whose temple-like facade faced the street, though the main entrance was located on one side, and the Little Rock High School, a monumental Arkansas school building for its era, which was later expanded by the addition of a large auditorium and gymnasium designed by George Mann.

Fig. 84 George R. Mann was Charles Thompson's most distinguished peer in the Arkansas architectural community at the turn of the century.

68

Fig. 85 The interior of the "new" Pulaski County Courthouse exemplifies George Mann's attention to detail and his fondness of classical spaces.

Fig. 86 Architect Frank Gibb's home in Little Rock presents a Greek-temple-like facade to Arch Street.

Fig. 87 The Arlington Hotel in Hot Springs was one of George Mann's last commissions. His design partner on the project was Eugene Stern.

In 1903, Gibb had enough work as an architect to employ two draftsmen, Theodore M. Sanders and Frank J. Ginocchio. Sanders had studied architecture at the University of Illinois at Urbana between 1898 and 1902.[5] He had also spent a year of study at the Ecole des Beaux Arts in Paris, the leading school of design in the world at the time. In addition to architecture, Sanders had studied art and sketching while in Paris. Perhaps it was the development of these creative skills which led Sanders, later in life, to prefer the process of designing a building to the labor of overseeing its construction.

When Sanders returned from Paris he married Irene Pareira and began his drafting job with Frank Gibb. Gibb was impressed with his talents and, in 1906, made him a partner. Together they are known to have designed the Ada Thompson Memorial Home and a house for H. M. Ramey in Little Rock. Gibb and Sanders worked together until 1910, when the younger man struck out on his own.[6]

For the next nine years, Sanders enjoyed an active architectural practice which was only temporarily set back by the death of his wife in 1916. He designed several schools for the Little Rock School Board, the Royal and Park Theaters, and a number of private residences. Sanders was conversant in the vocabularies of several styles: The Park Theater was a rich display of Beaux Arts Classicism, the Woodruff School a restrained exercise in institutional Prairie, and the Cornish House a picturesque mixture of Tudor and Craftsman.[7]

70

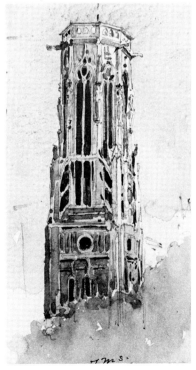

Theodore Sanders (left, Fig. 88) was a dashing young man when he travelled to Paris in the early 20th Century to study design at the Ecole des Beaux Arts. The French capital inspired a collection of sketchwork and watercolors (below, Figs. 89 and 90).

Fig. 91 Theodore Sanders and Frank Gibb collaborated on the 1909 Colonial Revival design for the Ada Thompson Memorial Home in Little Rock.

72

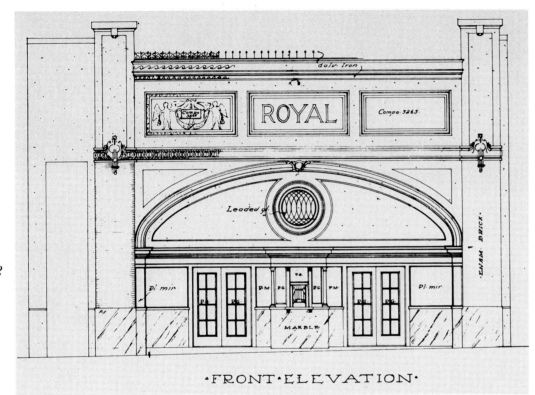

·FRONT·ELEVATION·

Theodore Sanders was a talented designer whose plans for the Royal (above, Fig. 92) and the Park (right, Fig. 93)Theaters represented some of the best commercial architecture of its age.

Fig. 94 For the Cornish House in Little Rock, Theodore Sanders married stone, brick, stucco, wood, glass, and tile to create a large home of remarkable warmth and character.

Gibb's other draftsman, Frank Ginocchio, worked for him until 1905, when he left to join Charles Thompson's firm.[8] Only a teenager, Ginocchio worked diligently as a draftsman and soon decided he wanted to pursue a career in architecture. In 1906, he left Thompson to obtain a formal education in architecture at the University of Illinois.[9]

When Ginocchio returned to Little Rock in 1910, he was assigned to the staff supervising the construction of the new state capitol. Subsequently, he rejoined Thompson's office and stayed until World War I. Ginocchio brought fresh design ideas to the firm and may have urged Thompson to employ such avant-garde architectural forms as the Prairie style on commissions like the Al Amin Temple. He was also an experienced field man and was later named Supervising Architect for Construction for the Thompson firm.

In addition to Ginocchio and Harding, Thompson was fortunate by 1913 to have in his employ John Parks Almand. Like Mann, Almand was a professionally trained architect who had received his schooling on the East Coast. After a short post-graduation assignment in Cuba, he came to Little Rock and joined Thompson's firm, where he worked for three years. From 1915 to the late 1960s, Almand enjoyed a long and mostly solo career as an architect in central Arkansas. Though he was responsible for many beautiful Methodist churches throughout the state, his most memorable project was the design of Little Rock Central High School in 1926.[10]

Upon the outbreak of World War I, Ginocchio was called to service in the military and placed in the Army Corps of Engineers under the direction of Colonel John R. Fordyce. During the war, he was the architect in charge of constructing Camp Pike (now Camp Robinson) in North Little Rock and Jefferson Barracks in St. Louis.[11] Ginocchio returned to Little Rock at the conclusion of the hostilities, hoping to pick up where he had left off. But since Tom Harding was now a partner in the Thompson firm, Ginocchio decided he would seek his fortune elsewhere.

In 1919, the two fellow draftsmen, Theo Sanders and Frank Ginocchio, formed a partnership. They made a strong combination — Sanders' interest in design complemented Ginocchio's ability to supervise construction. Like other architects of the period, they frequently made use of the variety of revival styles which were popular in the early twentieth century. The First Presbyterian Church in Newport was executed in Italian Renaissance, while the Second Presbyterian Church in Little Rock was designed in the traditional Gothic Revival style. Sanders and Ginocchio were also responsible for a large number of private residences, most in the provincial styles popular in America in the early 1920s.

In addition to achieving professional success, Sanders and Ginocchio's personal lives prospered as well. In 1924 Ginocchio married Bess Rogoski; in the same year Sanders remarried, this time to Annette Joseph. Sanders' happiness was short-lived, though, for his new bride soon suffered a crippling stroke and spent the rest of her life an invalid.[12]

The Safferstone House in Little Rock (right, Fig. 95) was an unusual Mission Revival residence designed by Theo Sanders and Frank Ginocchio in 1925. John Parks Almand (far right, Fig. 96) was a skilled architect who worked for Thompson between 1913 and 1915.

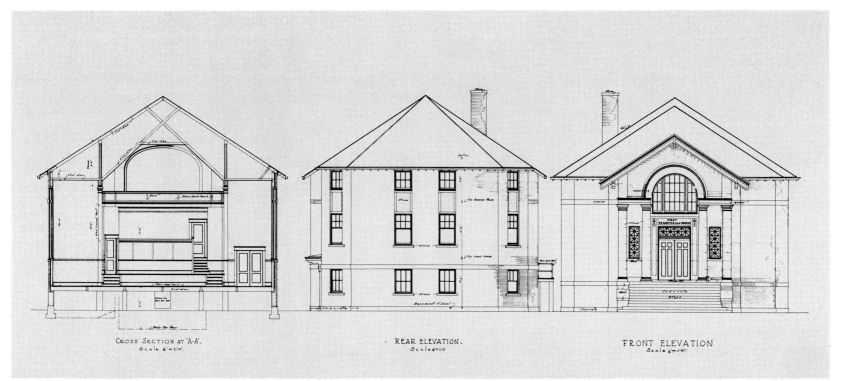

CROSS SECTION AT 'A-A'.
Scale ¼" = 1'-0".

REAR ELEVATION.
Scale ¼" = 1'-0"

FRONT ELEVATION
Scale ¼" = 1'-0"

75

Fig. 97 The First Presbyterian Church of Newport, shown here in front and rear elevation, as well as cross-section, was completed shortly after Theodore Sanders and Frank Ginocchio became partners in 1919.

During this same post-war period, the architectural firm of Thompson & Harding continued to actively participate in the rapid growth of Arkansas. They were practicing in the city of El Dorado when oil was discovered in Union County in the early 1920s. The firm established an office there and affiliated with local architect L. Wilsey Hunter. Among the clients who Thompson and Harding served was Charles Murphy, one of the men whose fortune was built on oil and natural gas, for whom they designed an impressive home. They also prepared the plans for El Dorado High School and other landmark structures throughout the area.[13]

Thompson's expectation of securing large commercial and public projects, which had been the original impetus to enter into a partnership with Harding, was never fully realized. While the firm did design the Federal Reserve and Exchange National Banks in Little Rock, as well as numerous school buildings, the majority of its commissions were for small businesses and residences.

Harding designed many homes and enlarged the repertoire of styles for the firm. He was a perfectionist who liked being involved in the entire design process from conception through development to construction. Harding often insisted on doing his own drafting work to ensure that each detail was properly rendered. The residences he designed bear witness to his creativity and preference for "humanely scaled" buildings.

Though the Prairie, Craftsman, and Classical styles declined in popularity after World War I, Harding incorporated their picturesque design qualities and low-rise forms into the various "period revival" homes the Thompson firm designed in the 1920s. The great war had exposed many American servicemen to the provincial architecture of Europe and, upon returning home, they were keen on owning their own Tudor cottages, Spanish haciendas, and Dutch colonial farmhouses.

Fig. 98 El Dorado High School was one of four buildings designed by the Thompson firm for that city's school board during the 1920s when his office was affiliated with local architect L. Wilsey Hunter.

76

Fig. 99 The Federal Reserve Bank Building in Little Rock features enormous brass doors and a Spartan neo-classical facade. It was designed by Thompson and Harding in 1924.

The Dorsey McRae House in Hope (opposite page, Fig. 100), the Mrs. J. B. Hurley House in Warren (above, Fig. 101), and the A. E. McLean House in Little Rock (right, Fig. 102) are typical of the period-revival style residences which the Thompson & Harding firm designed after World War I.

These period-revival residences were designed to be quaint and informal, and generally were planned for comfortable and convenient living in an age without servants. The Dorsey McRae House in Hope, the A. E. McLean House in Little Rock, and the J. B. Hurley House in Warren were all typical designs by the Thompson firm during the decade following World War I.

While the styles remained traditional, early twentieth-century architects like Thompson and Harding often found themselves having to accommodate an altogether new factor in their designs — the automobile. Not only did it change lifestyles, create an elaborate network of highways across the country, and alter the urban environment, it demanded new building types. First and foremost was the filling station, and Thompson and Harding designed one of Arkansas's first in the Hillcrest area of Little Rock. In Warren, Henry Thane commissioned the firm to draw plans for a building which served two separate dealers, each with his own showroom and shop.

The architectural profession was changing, too. The design and construction of structures of all types had become big business in America. The expanding need for shelter forced ever greater standardization of building components and procedures. As a result, architects found themselves spending less effort on designing custom features and more time on efficient construction management.

In this profit-minded environment, the Thompson firm excelled. The office was well regulated and strictly managed, opening at 8:00 a.m. and closing at 5:00 p.m. Thompson expected proficiency from his employees, but did not demand that they follow his example of long work hours. In fact, no overtime was permitted.[14] Business finances were kept in strict order, enabling Thompson to meet his payroll and cover any debts incurred by the firm. This efficiency and discipline helped to ensure the dedication of his staff and inspired confidence in prospective clients.

79

The well-managed office permitted Thompson to become involved in a variety of activities outside the firm. He served as vice-president for the Thibault Milling Company, Plunkett-Jarrell Company, Voss-Hutton Company, and Union Trust Bank. He was also a board member of the Little Rock Chamber of Commerce and the Little Rock Country Club, as well as the chairman of the Donaghey Foundation and the Pulaski County Red Cross.[15]

Thompson also helped to foster the development and improvement of the architectural profession in Arkansas. In the winter of 1921, he participated in a series of meetings which, that April, led to the founding of an Arkansas Chapter of the American Institute of Architects. After the chapter's establishment, Thompson was elected to its first executive committee.[16]

(text continues on page 85)

Fig. 103 Thompson and Harding designed a "split dealership" for Henry Thane's two automobile businesses in Warren.

80

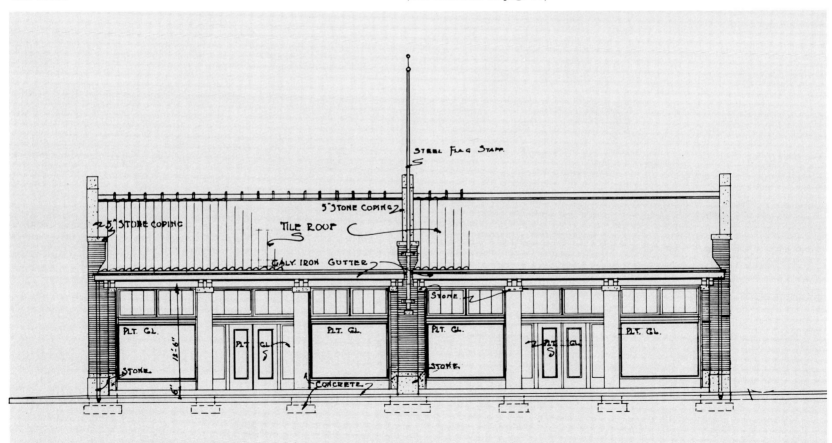

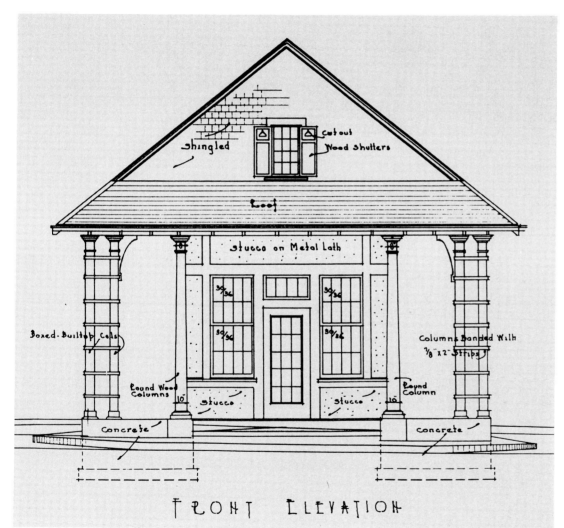

Fig. 104 Automobiles created a number of new building types in America, including the filling station. Thompson and Harding designed one of the first in Arkansas for the Hillcrest neighborhood of Little Rock in 1924.

Charles Thompson's commitment to a well-ordered, well-regulated life did not stop at his office door; life in the Thompson household was equally structured. Son-in-law Edwin Cromwell recalls that meals did not vary from week to week, and that on Sunday mornings waffles were served. One time, Thompson's son George was home visiting from Vanderbilt. George, who was especially fond of waffles, was to leave on Saturday to pick up a friend in Memphis. Mrs. Thompson broke with the schedule and on Saturday morning fixed waffles as a treat for her son. Mr. Thompson, when he came downstairs and discovered waffles on the table, immediately returned to his bedroom and put on his Sunday suit.

Fig. 105 St. Paul Parish Church in Batesville, designed by the Thompson firm in 1916.

Fig. 106 The R. A. Dowdy Building on Main Street in Batesville is notable for its workmanlike use of native stone and brick. Theodore Sanders was its architect.

Fig. 107 The Arkadelphia School was designed by Thompson and Harding in 1917. Its Prairie-School-like shape and banding was combined with a classically inspired entrance.

During his many years of association with Charles Thompson, Thomas Harding's professional skills and reputation became highly regarded. Thompson had always encouraged his young draftsmen and architects to advance their own careers and was not surprised when Harding asked to dissolve their partnership in 1925. While Harding confidently opened his own office, Thompson realized his advancing age and diversified activities could potentially weaken his firm's architectural practice. He began to feel "the need of younger men to carry on" and began to investigate the possibility of merging his office with another.[17]

Thompson was pleased to see his former employee, Frank Ginocchio, enjoying a measure of success with his partner, Theo Sanders. The two firms decided to combine efforts, and the partnership of Thompson, Sanders & Ginocchio was announced on September 8, 1927.[18] This professional association, which lasted over ten years, would be the last in Charles Thompson's fifty-two year architectural practice. ✖

85

Fig. 108 The Merchants and Planters Bank in Clarendon is a handsome commercial building of period-revival design. Thompson and Harding were its architects in 1921.

CHAPTER FIVE

THOMPSON, SANDERS & GINOCCHIO

The firm of Charles Thompson, Theo Sanders, and Frank Ginocchio enjoyed a fortunate combination of skills and experience. Thompson, due to the length and breadth of his service to Arkansas, was well-known and respected. Sanders was a highly regarded designer familiar with the vocabulary of many architectural styles. Ginocchio was a strong supervising architect for construction whose skills helped to ensure the timely completion of the firm's projects. In addition to their professional expertise, each partner's social and religious contacts — Thompson was an Episcopalian, Sanders a Jew, and Ginocchio a Catholic — brought business to the office and helped the firm prosper in an era of extraordinary economic uncertainty.

The Union Trust Company Building in Little Rock (opposite page, Fig. 109) was the most remarkable Art Deco structure in Arkansas. The 1929 bank featured extensive geometric ornamentation, stylized figure sculpture, and metal grillwork (right, Fig. 110). The Union Trust Building, together with the terra-cotta faced building to its right, were destroyed in the 1970s to create a parking lot.

The firm's active involvement in civic affairs also brought it into contact with many potential future clients. In 1927, for example, the most devastating flood in Arkansas history had left many homeless and penniless. Thompson raised money to feed and clothe those left destitute by the flood and designed cabins to replace homes that had been destroyed. For these efforts, he was voted Little Rock's "Most Useful Citizen" in 1927.[1]

Despite Arkansas's slumping agricultural economy, Little Rock was in the midst of a building boom when the practice of Thompson, Sanders & Ginocchio began during the last years of the Roaring Twenties. This was the heyday of the city's Main Street, when it served as a shopping center for the entire state. Hotels such as the LaFayette and the Albert Pike were constructed to accommodate guests who regularly travelled to Little Rock to conduct their public and private business. And banks like Union Trust erected new buildings to reflect their growing importance in the community.

The Union Trust Building was one of the most avant-garde projects executed by the Thompson, Sanders & Ginocchio firm. Constructed in 1929, this structure was easily the finest, most monumental example of Art Deco architecture in Arkansas. Influenced by the ornamentation of the buildings at the 1925 Exposition Des Arts Decoratifs in Paris, the Union Trust Bank abandoned all allusions to earlier building styles. It distinctively combined complex metal and stonework decoration with a box-like limestone mass. No other "moderne" structure in the state ever quite rivalled its scale or attention to detail.

Shortly after the completion of the Union Trust Building, the local economy began to nose-dive. The 1929 stock-market crash and the subsequent economic depression of the 1930s had a tremendous impact on business activities of all kinds. The banking industry was especially hard hit, and when the American Exchange Bank threatened to go under, Thompson worked tirelessly to prevent its collapse. Thompson also headed the Community Chest Fund of 1930 and selflessly contributed his time and talents to efforts of all kinds to bolster local services facing financial failure.[2]

Fred Heiskell, the long-time publisher of the *Arkansas Gazette,* wrote of Thompson's work in 1931:

> He was leading in an effort to reopen the closed American Exchange Bank which was the largest in Arkansas. His Red Cross work was a brilliant success and while he says he has failed in the bank matter, if the bank is ultimately opened, it will be due to the foundation work Charlie did. Charlie has become one of the leading and most useful citizens of Little Rock and of Arkansas. He did splendid work during the war. Then he served as head of the Chamber of Commerce and now he is called upon in any big emergency.[3]

In 1930, the United States Treasury Department approved funds for a new post office and federal courthouse in Little Rock. Arkansas architects, who were badly in need of work, were outraged when their design proposals were rejected because the Treasury Department was not accustomed to associating with local architects on projects under three million dollars. Thompson, among others, corresponded repeatedly with Senators Joseph T. Robinson and T. H. Caraway, Congressman Heartsill Ragon, and the supervising architect at the Treasury Department, voicing his strong objections to the plans for the new post office and the government's construction policy. At the height of the controversy, representatives from six local architectural firms met in Thompson's office to draft a petition asking that the exterior design be changed.[4]

Despite these objections, the post office was constructed as planned and without assistance from local architects. However, legislation was soon passed to prevent similar occurrences in the future. Despite this appeasement, though, eighteen architects — including Thompson, Sanders, and Ginocchio — issued a statement calling for the creation of an Arkansas Board of Architects. Failure to be registered with the board, they argued, would prevent a designer from working within the state.[5] Though it required nearly a decade to enact the necessary state statutes, their eventual success in 1939 was still another sign of the increasing professionalization of Arkansas's architectural community.

Theodore Sanders (above left, Fig. 111) and Frank Ginocchio (above right, Fig. 112) merged their architectural practice with Charles L. Thompson's office in the late 1920s. Their talents and backgrounds make it possible for the firm to prosper during the Great Depression.

Fig. 113 The Hot Spring County Courthouse in Malvern, designed by Thompson, Sanders, & Ginocchio, was one of many commissions the firm received for public buildings in the 1930s. Its W.P.A. Moderne style stands in stark contrast to Thompson's ornate turn-of-the-century courthouses.

90

Religious and educational structures were welcome projects when private construction declined during the Depression. St. Francis Parish in Forrest City (opposite page, Fig. 114) was a modest adaptation of the traditional architecture for which Thompson and his associates had become renowned. The Christ the King Church in Fort Smith (above, Fig. 115) was a simple design constructed of field stone.

The lean years of the 1930s forced some significant changes on the building design profession as a whole, and on the Thompson firm in particular. Fewer and fewer people were commissioning architects to design custom homes and, when they did, the results were often uncreative reinterpretations of historic building styles. For example, El Dorado's R. N. Garrett House was a modified Georgian residence, while the H. D. Hundling House in Little Rock was reminiscent of an eighteenth-century New England farmhouse.

To an ever-greater degree, the most lucrative projects of major design firms like Thompson, Sanders & Ginocchio were the institutional and commercial commissions. Churches and schools kept the office busy during the 1930s and gave the architects a chance to do some of their best work. The Parish House for Little Rock's Christ Episcopal Church was one of several ecclesiastical projects adeptly given a Gothic-style treatment. The campuses at present-day Philander Smith College and the University of Arkansas at Pine Bluff were graced by buildings in the Georgian and Renaissance Revival styles, respectively. Some commercial projects allowed the firm to dabble in other historic styles. For a building for M. B. Moore in Little Rock, the architects — perhaps influenced by California buildings of the Twenties and the extravagant sets in popular motion pictures — employed Spanish Colonial styling, an unusual choice for an Arkansas structure in the Depression years.

92

Mount St. Mary's Academy in Little Rock (opposite page, Fig. 116), shown in an aerial view taken c. World War II, presented Thompson with an outstanding site to practice monumental architecture. The convent building, its additions, and the gymnasium were all designed by his firm. Arkansas Agricultural, Mechanical & Normal School (right, Fig. 117), today UAPB, blended traditional architectural forms with the emerging decorative elements of Art Moderne.

94

At left, the Park Hotel in Hot Springs (Fig. 118); above, the North Little Rock Post Office (Fig. 119); and next page, the Little Rock Boys Club (Fig. 120). All three buildings were designed in the early 1930s by Thompson, Sanders & Ginocchio.

96

In January of 1938, Charles Thompson — now almost seventy years old and desirous of more leisure hours to devote to his many personal interests — announced his retirement after fifty-two years of active practice. In a statement to the *Arkansas Democrat,* he assured past and future clients, "Mr. Sanders and Mr. Ginocchio will carry on the work without interruption and will serve our many friends in Arkansas faithfully as well."[6]

Thompson left the firm, but not the service of his community. In April 1938, Governor Carl Bailey appointed him to the chairmanship of the State Planning Commission; he filled the unexpired term of friend and former governor George Donaghey, who had died several months earlier. Thompson was also president of the Chamber of Commerce, played a key role on the Little Rock Water Commission by arguing for the creation of the Lake Maumelle reservoir, and led the campaign to secure the funds necessary to build a city auditorium. He was later asked to design the new facility, but declined the honor because of his role in its promotion.[7] In addition to these public duties, Thompson continued to sit on the board of directors of several firms and private philanthropic organizations until very late in his life. He was widely and warmly eulogized upon his death on December 30, 1959, at age 91.[8] 🐾

97

Thompson, Sanders & Ginocchio employed a wide variety of styles in the residences and commercial buildings designed during their partnership. The impressively scaled and designed J. Merrick Moore House in Little Rock (opposite page, Fig. 121) contrasts with the modest, traditionally styled home of R. N. Garrett, Jr., in El Dorado (above, Fig. 122). The M. B. Moore Building in Little Rock (left, Fig. 123) is a rare example of the firm's use of Mediterranean Revival architecture.

CHAPTER SIX

EPILOGUE

Theodore Sanders and Frank Ginocchio continued with the architectural firm until 1941, when Sanders withdrew from the partnership, leaving the office to the younger man. That same year, three months before the bombing of Pearl Harbor, Edwin B. Cromwell was invited into the firm to succeed Sanders. A graduate of Princeton University, Cromwell had begun his practice in the Philadelphia office of Charles Z. Klauder. In 1935, he had come to Arkansas as an architect with the Resettlement Administration. From 1936 to 1941, he had practiced with the firm of Wittenberg & Delony of Little Rock. When Cromwell joined Ginocchio at the outbreak of World War II, he and his partner divided the office duties; Cromwell assumed responsibility for the "inside work" — design, drafting, and business management — while Ginocchio stuck with the construction supervision he knew so well. Their architectural office was given high-priority military work; indeed, for the next five years most of the firm's commissions were for projects in support of the war effort.

Ginocchio and Cromwell were chiefly responsible for providing their firm with a strong sense of continuity from the 1940s to the 1960s. But there were other faithful employees who helped to ensure consistency and quality to the architectural

The Arkansas Governor's Mansion in Little Rock (opposite page, Fig. 124) was a project undertaken by the partnership of Frank Ginocchio and Edwin B. Cromwell. The building's traditional design was typical of their office's work in the 1940s. Cromwell (above, Fig. 125), who joined Ginocchio shortly before the outbreak of World War II, was an essential source of continuity for the firm's activities after the retirement of Thompson and Ginocchio.

practice begun by Bartlett and Thompson. Percy deVerne Burton, first employed by the firm in 1908, continued to produce plans for Colonial-style churches with graceful steeples through the 1950s. W. Hal Phelps, a graduate of Texas A&M who joined the office before Thompson left, stayed until 1952. Fannie Mae Howland, who had started as a secretary, progressed to the business and specification department, where she was a valuable employee for many years. When she retired in 1950, she had contributed almost half a century to the firm.

Following the war, the firm expanded to serve its growing industrial clientele. Among the professionals who joined the firm and later became partners were Charles Carter, John J. Truemper, Jr., Robert H. Millett, Dietrich Neyland and Ben Dees. Carter, a former architect with the Federal Housing Administration, eventually served as secretary-treasurer of the firm, a post he held at the time of his death in 1969. Truemper, educated at the University of Illinois, started at the firm as a student draftsman; he eventually rose to president and chairman of the board. Millett, also a one-time draftsman, received his formal training at the Massachusetts Institute of Technology and achieved widespread recognition for his brilliance in industrial building design.

Dietrich Neyland joined the firm in 1950 and began its confident employment of the progressive glass and metal vocabulary of the new International style. Neyland came to the office from Shreveport, Louisiana, where he had designed a high school featured in *Life* magazine as an example of the new post-war architecture. A former designer for famed Viennese architect Richard Neutra, Neyland soon influenced the direction of high-style architecture throughout Arkansas through his development of glass curtain-wall technology and interior space planning. He also served as both president and chairman of the firm.

Eventually, the increasing number of industrial and governmental commissions required the creation of an engineering department. First, in 1954, with the hiring of Ben Dees, then in 1956 with Oliver Gatchell, and again in 1960 with William Woodsmall, the firm moved towards the systematic integration of its engineering capacity with its architectural design capabilities. Dees, Gatchell, and Woodsmall later became full partners, perhaps the first engineers to enjoy such status in

100

The KTHV-Channel 11 television station in Little Rock (above, Fig. 126) was one of the state's first "glass curtain wall" buildings designed by Dietrich Neyland. Neyland's contributions to contemporary architecture in Arkansas spanned over a quarter-century and included the Little Rock Regional Airport terminal building (right, Fig. 127).

an Arkansas architectural firm since the days of Rickon and Thompson.

This multidisciplinary character made it possible for the firm to take a leading role in several major construction projects between the mid-1950s and the 1970s. These included the Little Rock Regional Airport, Little Rock University (later the University of Arkansas at Little Rock), and Maumelle New Town. Eugene P. Levy, a University of Virginia graduate whose interest in governmental facility design had a clear impact on the firm's master plan for the Arkansas State Capitol complex, and Ray K. Parker, who later directed the management and construction administration divisions, joined the firm during this time and eventually became senior partners, too.

As it nears its one-hundredth birthday, the design firm of Cromwell, Truemper, Levy, Parker & Woodsmall continues to be a major force in the practice of architecture in Arkansas. Indeed, a substantial number of its award-winning projects lie beyond the boundaries of state; some are overseas. While time and changing fashion now make many of the firm's buildings appear dated, a remarkable number survive as legitimate landmarks — silent testimony to their continuing usefulness and quality.

Meanwhile, the firm's size and capabilities are a tribute to the talents, personalities, and perseverance of the many distinguished partners and employees who have served it during the last century. In particular, the five decades Charles Thompson and Frank Ginocchio invested in this firm, and the four more by Edwin Cromwell, are the necessary thread of continuity so important to the delivery of professional services and creation of dependable products.

As the passage of time permits us to view his accomplishments in an increasingly objective light, it is difficult not to conclude that Charles L. Thompson's most important contribution to his profession was not his designs, but the found-

101

ing and perpetuating of an "architectural association." From his shaky partnership with Benjamin Bartlett, Thompson built a legacy which has survived wars, depressions, changes in partners, and the enormous evolution of the architectural profession itself. It is a monument, of a kind, which appears likely to survive as long as the buildings themselves. ❧

The Cromwell firm was involved in the planning and construction of the campus of the University of Arkansas at Little Rock for over two decades. One of the many buildings it designed was the main library (Fig. 128).

CHAPTER TWO: THE EARLY PARTNERSHIPS

1. Quapaw Quarter Association, "Little Rock's First Architect," QQA Preservation Resource Center.
2. Quapaw Quarter Association, "Larrimore, R. — Architect," QQA Preservation Resource Center.
3. *Little Rock City Directory* (Little Rock: Price & Barton, 1871), pp. 70, 79.
4. Ira Don Richards, *Story of a Rivertown* (Benton, Arkansas: Ira Don Richards, 1969), pp. 99-100.
5. Quapaw Quarter Association, "Notes on the 1880s and 1890s," QQA Preservation Resource Center.
6. *Arkansas Gazette,* 18 September 1915.
7. *Census of Polk County, Iowa* (Des Moines: 1880).
8. *Arkansas Gazette,* 15 September 1885 and 14 November 1937.
9. *Arkansas Gazette,* 15 September 1885.
10. *Arkansas Gazette,* 14 August 1887.
11. *Arkansas Gazette,* 14 September 1939.
12. *Who's Who Publishers* (Little Rock: New Era Press, 1921), p. 129.
13. *Arkansas Gazette,* 23 June 1957.
14. *Transactions,* vol. 2 (Little Rock: Arkansas Society of Engineers, Architects, and Surveyors, 1888), p. 5.
15. *Transactions,* vol. 2 (1888), p. 20.
16. *Transactions,* vol. 1 (1887), pp. 9-16, 56-60.
17. *Transactions,* vol. 2 (1888), p. 20.
18. *Transactions,* vol. 2 (1888), p. 5.
19. *Arkansas Gazette,* 23 June 1957; Interview with Edwin B. Cromwell and Charles L. Thompson, Jr., 1980.
20. Interview with Charles L. Thompson, Jr., 1980.
21. Interview with Edwin B. Cromwell, 1980.
22. *Arkansas Gazette,* 14 September 1939 and 31 December 1959.
23. *Arkansas Gazette,* 31 December 1979; Interview with Cromwell.
24. "Contract for Partnership Agreement," 15 January 1891, Edwin B. Cromwell Collection.
25. *A New Year's Greeting* (Little Rock: Rickon & Thompson, Architects, 1895).
26. "Contract for Partnership Dissolution," 14 April 1897, Cromwell Collection.

CHAPTER THREE: CHARLES L. THOMPSON, ARCHITECT

1. Interview with Cromwell.
2. Interview with Virginia Burton Russell, 1980.
3. *Little Rock City Directory* (Little Rock: Arkansas Democrat Company, 1906), p. 134.
4. Henrietta Thompson, Inventory of books in Charles L. Thompson's personal library, 1934, Cromwell Collection. Thompson's personal library contained over 600 volumes spanning historical works to serious fiction to astronomy and archaeology; it is now at the University of Arkansas at Little Rock.
5. *Goodspeed Biographical and Historical Memoirs of Central Arkansas* (Chicago: Goodspeed Publishing Company, 1889), pp. 510-511.
6. Interview with Thompson.
7. *Quapaw Quarter: A Guide to Little Rock's 19th Century Neighborhoods* (Little Rock: Quapaw Quarter Association, 1976).
8. Interview with Henrietta Thompson Cromwell, 1980. Mary Watkins Thompson was the daughter of Dr. Clairbourne Watkins and the granddaughter of Arkansas Supreme Court Justice George C. Watkins.
9. George W. Donaghey, *Building a State Capitol* (Little Rock: Parke-Harper Company, 1937), p. 228.
10. Interview with Tom Harding III and Pat Harding, 1980. Harding's sons remember that he was fascinated by firefighting equipment and invented a device to isolate fires within buildings. The city of Little Rock eventually named him an Honorary Fire Chief.
11. From Tom Harding's registration form, Arkansas State Board of Architects, 1939.

CHAPTER FOUR: COLLEAGUES AND COMPETITORS

1. George R. Mann, "At the Request of My Daughters...," 1932 MS, pp. 3-4.
2. Mann, pp. 5-10.
3. Mann, pp. 10-11.
4. Col. A. J. Almand, letter to V. Starr Mitchell, 11 January 1978, QQA Preservation Resource Center.
5. Interview with Charles Witsell, Jr., 1981.
6. From Theodore M. Sanders' registration form, Arkansas State Board of Architects, 1939.
7. *Little Rock City Directory* (Little Rock: Arkansas Democrat Company, 1910), p. 467.
8. Inventory of drawings in Charles L. Thompson Collection.
9. *Little Rock City Directory* (Little Rock: Arkansas Democrat Company, 1903-1904), p. 239.
10. Interview with Bess Ginocchio, Little Rock, 1980.
11. *Arkansas Gazette,* 8 September 1927.
12. From the records of Sparks Manor Nursing Home in Fort Smith, Arkansas, 1974.
13. From L. Wilsey Hunter's registration form, Arkansas State Board of Architects, 1939.
14. Interview with Cromwell.
15. *Arkansas Gazette,* 31 December 1959.
16. Articles of Incorporation and Other Materials Related to the Establishment of the Arkansas Chapter of the American Institute of Architects, 1921, QQA Preservation Resource Center.
17. *Arkansas Gazette,* 8 September 1927.
18. *Arkansas Gazette,* 8 September 1927.

CHAPTER FIVE: THOMPSON, SANDERS & GINOCCHIO

1. *Arkansas Gazette,* 31 December 1959.
2. *Arkansas Gazette,* 8 September 1927.
3. Fred Heiskell, letter to Mrs. C. M. Shirk, 14 March 1931, Cromwell Collection.
4. *Arkansas Democrat,* 8 July 1931.
5. *Arkansas Democrat,* 8 July 1931.
6. *Arkansas Democrat,* 18 January 1938.
7. *Arkansas Gazette,* 14 September 1939.
8. *Arkansas Gazette,* 31 December 1959.

CATALOGUE TO BUILDINGS BY
CHARLES L. THOMPSON AND ASSOCIATES

What follows is a complete list of all the projects represented in the Charles L. Thompson and Associates archives, located at Arkansas's Old State House Museum in Little Rock, along with a handful of designs which have been documented to be the work of these gentlemen from other sources.

In the collection, there are approximately 2,500 projects on almost 25,000 individual sheets. Approximately 65% of the plans are ink on linen; 20% are blueprint, blueline, or other form of reproduction; 10% are ink on vellum; and the balance are ink or pencil on tracing paper. Nearly all are construction plans, as opposed to design or development drawings.

A wide range of buildings are represented in the collection. Thirty-nine percent are residences, 36% are commercial buildings, 8% are schools, 8% are public buildings such as courthouses, post offices, or armories, 5% are churches or religious structures, and 4% are civic or institutional buildings. The drawings span the time from the late 1880s to the late 1930s, with 10% dated before 1900, 75% between 1900 and 1930, and 15% between 1930 and 1938.

The drawings have been stacked on shelves, rolled up, and placed in paper sacks. Most of the linen plans are in very good condition. The ones on vellum or tracing paper are brittle and break apart or crack when unrolled. The blueprints are hard to unroll and crumble to the touch.

Many of the projects included in the archives were executed when the architect was not directly associated with the Thompson firm. For example, the plans for the Ada Thompson House, completed in 1909 by Frank Gibb and Theodore Sanders, were added to the collection when Thompson, Sanders, and Frank Ginocchio formed their partnership in the 1920s.

In addition to being an index to the Thompson archives, this catalogue is the product of an extensive search throughout Arkansas to identify the remaining buildings and document those structures known to have been designed by Thompson and his associates, but which are not represented in the collection by a set of plans. The research team found many buildings in the state that closely resembled those designed by the firm, but the structures for which no architect could be assigned were not included.

The catalogue is alphabetically ordered first by county, then by city, and lastly by client. From left to right are listed the client, the building or project, the architect, the date of design, and the structure's address, regardless of whether it is still standing.

The **client** is the original party who commissioned the drawings; it may be an individual, organization, or governmental agency. The **building** and **project** include first, the type of structure and then second, the kind of project it represented. The former is normally spelled out, with the exception of residential which is abbreviated "R." The latter includes new construction ("nc"), additions ("add"), alterations ("alt."), and some combinations.

The client entry is occasionally marked with either one or two asterisks. A single asterisk ("*") denotes a property which was part of the 1982 thematic nomination of structures to the National Register of Historic Places. A double asterisk ("**") denotes its individual placement on the National Register prior to the thematic nomination.

Under the category of **architect**, there is a number of different partnerships. They are:

BB — Benjamin Bartlett
B&T — Bartlett & Thompson
CT — Charles L. Thompson
FR — Fred Rickon
R&T — Rickon & Thompson
G&S — Gibb & Sanders
S&G — Sanders & Ginocchio
T&H — Thompson & Harding
TH — Thomas Harding, Jr.
TS — Theodore Sanders
TS&G — Thompson, Sanders & Ginocchio

The **date** of design was indicated on the drawings or was determined through research; an approximate date is preceded by circa ("c."). The **address** records its known place of construction; if an exact address was not found through research, it was omitted. The absence of an address can also mean that the structure could not be located, was moved, never built, or destroyed.

Given the sheer number of projects known to have been executed by Thompson and his associates, it is reasonable to believe that interested researchers and property owners may continue to discover Thompson buildings not represented in the archives for many years. The Quapaw Quarter Association is anxious to receive information which may lead to the documentation of additional Thompson projects, as well as any corrections to work which has already been done. These updates will be collected and turned over to the Old State House Museum, the repository for the Thompson archives, as well as assembled for inclusion into the republication of this book now planned for 1985, the centennial of the architectural firm of Cromwell, Truemper, Levy, Parker & Woodsmall. If you have such additions, changes, or leads to new information, please contact the Quapaw Quarter Association through P. O. Box 1104, Little Rock, Arkansas 72203.

CLIENT	BLDG-PROJECT	ARCHITECT	DATE	ADDRESS

ARKANSAS COUNTY

DEWITT

CLIENT	BLDG-PROJECT	ARCHITECT	DATE	ADDRESS
DeWitt Meth. Church	Church-nc	T&H	1925	303 W. Cross
First Nat'l Bank	Bank-add	CT	1914	Cross & Center St.
Garot, Leon	R-nc	TS&G	1936	
Home State Bank	Bank-nc	CT		
Park, Dr. C. E.	R-nc	CT	1914	Jefferson & First

STUTTGART

CLIENT	BLDG-PROJECT	ARCHITECT	DATE	ADDRESS
John Cain Park	R-nc	TS&G	1934	
Oaklawn Cemetery	Mausoleum-nc			

ASHLEY COUNTY

HAMBURG

CLIENT	BLDG-PROJECT	ARCHITECT	DATE	ADDRESS
Ashley County	Courthouse-nc	T&H	1923	
Watson Hardware	Comm-nc	TS		

PORTLAND

CLIENT	BLDG-PROJECT	ARCHITECT	DATE	ADDRESS
Dean, J. D.*	R-nc	CT		
Dean, J. D.	R-nc	CT		
Pugh, J. W.*	R-nc	CT	1904	
Pugh, T. R.	R-nc	CT	1916	

BOONE COUNTY

HARRISON

CLIENT	BLDG-PROJECT	ARCHITECT	DATE	ADDRESS
Boone Co.**	Courthouse-nc	CT	1909	
Boone Co.**	County Jail-nc	CT	1914	

BRADLEY COUNTY

HERMITAGE

CLIENT	BLDG-PROJECT	ARCHITECT	DATE	ADDRESS
Bank of Hermitage	Bank-nc	CT		

WARREN

CLIENT	BLDG-PROJECT	ARCHITECT	DATE	ADDRESS
Bradley Lumber	Store-nc	T&H	1920	
Dickenson, S. L.	Hotel add/alt	S&G		
Hughey, Mary E.	Store-nc	CT	1909	
Hurley, J. B.	R-nc	T&H	1917-1918	117 W. Pine
Thane, Henry	Auto bldg, nc	T&H	1919	
Thompson, W. T.	Hotel Sutherland-nc	CT	1910	
Warren Bank	Comm-alt	T&H	1917	
Wise, E. L.	R-nc	T&H	1921	116 Scotter St.

CALHOUN COUNTY

HAMPTON

CLIENT	BLDG-PROJECT	ARCHITECT	DATE	ADDRESS
Calhoun Co.	Bank-nc	S&G	1939	

CHICOT COUNTY

DERMOTT

CLIENT	BLDG-PROJECT	ARCHITECT	DATE	ADDRESS
Bank of Dermott	Bank-nc	CT		Iowa and Arkansas
Bordeaux, H.	R-nc	CT	1918	Main St.
Cohen, Joseph	Store-nc	CT	1909	
Crenshaw, A. C.	Store-nc	CT	1914	205 Iowa
Dente, Eli	Store-nc	CT	1914	
Dermott Grocery	Store-alt	T&H	1918	Arkansas Street
Dermott Grocery	Store-alt	T&H		
Dermott High School	Public-add	CT	1913	
Dermott School Bldg.	School-nc	CT	1908	

CLIENT	BLDG-PROJECT	ARCHITECT	DATE	ADDRESS
Dermott School Bldg.	Negro Sch.-nc	CT	1913	
Jones, J. F.	Store-nc	T&H	1920	
Kimpel, B. A.	Comm-nc	CT		
Thane and Remley	Store-nc	CT	1916	
Thane and Remley	Comm-nc	CT		
Walker, A. B.*	R-nc	CT	1918	606 Main

EUDORA

CLIENT	BLDG-PROJECT	ARCHITECT	DATE	ADDRESS
Dermott Grocery	Store-nc	T&H	1919	
Eudora School	High School-nc	TS&G	1928	
Feibleman, A.	Store-nc	T&H	1919	
Liberto & Protera	Store-nc	T&H	1920	
Merchants & Planters	Bank-nc	T&H	1917	
Meyer, Sol	R-nc	T&H	1919	

LAKE VILLAGE

CLIENT	BLDG-PROJECT	ARCHITECT	DATE	ADDRESS
Gaines Hardware Co.	Store-nc	CT	1904	
Lake Village School	School-nc	TS		
Vinson, Baldy	R-nc	CT		

CLARK COUNTY

ARKADELPHIA

CLIENT	BLDG-PROJECT	ARCHITECT	DATE	ADDRESS
Adams & Nowlin	Store-alt	T&H	1921	700-800 Clinton St.
Arkadelphia School*	School-nc	T&H	1917	11th Street at Pine & Haddock
Clark, J. G.	R-nc	CT	1907	
Clark Co.**	Courthouse		1899	Courthouse square
Crawford, J. H.	R-nc	CT	1890-1900	
McMillian, J. H.	R-nc	CT	1900-1910	
McMillian, J. H.	R-add/alt	T&H	1922	Corner Oak & McMillin
McNutt, Alice	R-nc	CT	1890-1900	

Fig. 129 Horace Mitchell House, Little Rock

104

CLIENT	BLDG-PROJECT	ARCHITECT	DATE	ADDRESS
McNutt, Alice	R-nc	CT		
Merchants & Farmers	Comm-nc	CT	1915	Sixth & Main
Patterson, J. W.	Store-nc	CT	1906	400-500 Main St.
Thomas, E. L.	R-nc	CT		
Women's Library Assn.**	Library-nc	CT	1900-1910	600-700 Caddo St.

GURDON

Neal's Brothers	Hotel & Bank-nc	CT	1900-1910	

PIGGOTT

Clay County	Courthouse-nc	CT	1899	
Houston College	School-nc	CT	1901	
Hunter, L.	R-nc	CT	1901	

CLEBURNE COUNTY

HEBER SPRINGS

Cleburne Co. Bank	Bank-nc	CT		Third and Main

CLEVELAND COUNTY

RISON

Cleveland Co.**	Courthouse-nc	TS	1910	

COLUMBIA COUNTY

MAGNOLIA

Columbia County*	Jail-nc		1910	205 W. Calhoun

Fig. 130 May-Marlar Grocer Building, Clarksville

CLIENT	BLDG-PROJECT	ARCHITECT	DATE	ADDRESS
State Agri School*	Boys' Dormitory-nc	TS	1910	Southern Arkansas University-Jackson Hall

WALDO

Bank of Waldo*	Bank-nc	CT	1907	Locust and Main
People's Bank	Bank-nc	CT	1923	

CONWAY COUNTY

MORRILTON

Burrow, Mrs. C.	R-nc	CT		
Coca-Cola Bottling*	Bottling plant-nc	TS&G	1929	211 No. Moose
Dewidle, T. A.	R-nc	CT		
First Nat'l Bank*	Bank	CT		Main at Moose
Frauenthal, Joe	R-nc	CT	1913	104 Deere
Halt, Fred	R-add/alt	CT	1916	101 West Church St.
Library Association**	County Library-nc	Harding	1916	101 West Church St.
Methodist Church	Sunday Sch./add	CT	1911	
Moore, J. S.	R-nc	CT		
Morrilton Baptist College	nc	R&T	c.1894	

CRAIGHEAD COUNTY

JONESBORO

Bank of Jonesboro	Bank-nc	CT		501 Union Street
Robertson, R. E.	Store-century bldg.-nc	CT	1899	
Robins & Robertson	Store-nc	CT	1901	
Warner, S. A., Jr.	R-nc	CT		

CRAWFORD COUNTY

ALMA

Bernays, Lewis	Store-nc	CT	1916	

CRITTENDON COUNTY

WEST MEMPHIS

Bishop of L.R.	Church-nc	TS&G		

DALLAS COUNTY

CARTHAGE

Bank of Carthage*	Bank-nc	CT	1907	

FORDYCE

Bank of Fordyce	Bank-nc	CT		223 Main St.
Bunn, W. J.	R-nc	CT		
Dallas County	Jail-nc	TS		
Fordyce Lumber Co.	Store-add/alt	TS&G		
Fordyce School Board	Training school-nc	CT		
Fordyce School Board	School-nc	CT		
Fordyce School Board	School-nc	CT	1905	
Fordyce School Board	School-nc	CT		
Gates, D. C.	R-nc	S&G		
Hampton, J. E.	R-nc	CT	1907	
Hampton, J. E.	R-nc	TS		
Home Insurance Co.*	Office-nc	CT	1908	300 Main
Home Insurance Co.	Comm-nc	CT		515 Oak Street
Kilgore Hotel Co.	Hotel-nc	TS&G	1928	
Kilgore Hotel Co.	Hotel-nc	TS&G	1928	
McKee, Charles	Bank & Store-nc	CT	1907	

CLIENT	BLDG-PROJECT	ARCHITECT	DATE	ADDRESS
McKee, Charles	Bank & store-nc	CT		
Parks, A. B.	Stable-nc	CT		600 Charlotte
Parks, A. B.	R-nc	CT		
Waters, D. A.*	R-nc	CT	1907	
Wynne, T. D.	R-nc	CT		

DESHA COUNTY

ARKANSAS CITY

CLIENT	BLDG-PROJECT	ARCHITECT	DATE	ADDRESS
Dedan, R.	Store-nc	CT		
Desha Bank & Trust	Bank-add/alt	CT	1911	
Dessent, J. S.	Store-nc	CT		
Thane, Henry*	R-nc	T&H	1919	Levy at First
Thane, Henry	Store-nc	CT		
Thane, Henry	R-nc	T&H		
Thompson, W. E.	R-nc	T&H	1920	

DUMAS

CLIENT	BLDG-PROJECT	ARCHITECT	DATE	ADDRESS
Bernhardt, I.	Store-nc	CT	1910	
Bernhardt, J.	Store-alt	CT	1914	
Bowles, Dr. T. H.	Store-nc	CT	1913	
Merchants & Farmer Bank*	Bank-nc	CT	1913	Waterman at Main
Porter, D. O.	R-nc	CT	1914	104 College
Porter, D. O.	Comm-nc	CT	1913	147 Waterman

MCGEHEE

CLIENT	BLDG-PROJECT	ARCHITECT	DATE	ADDRESS
Dessent, J. S.	Store-alt	TS&G	1930	
Dessent, J. S.	Comm-nc	TS&G	1930	
McGehee School Board	School-add	CT	1913	
McGehee School Board	School-nc	CT	1909	
McGehee Valley Bank	Bank-nc	CT	1913	
McGehee Valley Bank	Bank-nc	CT		
McGehee Valley Bank	Bank-add	CT	1913	
Thane, Henry	R-nc	T&H	1919	
Walchansky, Sam	R-nc	T&H	1920	

TILLAR

CLIENT	BLDG-PROJECT	ARCHITECT	DATE	ADDRESS
Ballard's Store				
Bank of Tillar (Henry Thane)	Bank-nc	CT	1915	

DREW COUNTY

MONTICELLO

CLIENT	BLDG-PROJECT	ARCHITECT	DATE	ADDRESS
Allen Hotel	Hotel-nc	TS		
Athre, Darwin	R-nc	CT		
Duke, C. T.	R-alt	CT	1910	
Erwin, B. Irma	R-nc	T&H	1925	
Congregation	Church-nc	TS		
AGRI School	School-nc	TS		
Winchester, Bank of	Bank-nc	CT		
Winchester School Board	School-nc	CT	1913	

FAULKNER COUNTY

CONWAY

CLIENT	BLDG-PROJECT	ARCHITECT	DATE	ADDRESS
Ark. State UCA Campus	Girls Dorm-alt	CT	1913	Parkway St.
Ark. State UCA Campus	Primary Sch-nc	CT	1913	Parkway St.
Ark. State UCA Campus	Barn-nc	CT		Parkway St.
Ark. State UCA Campus	Girls dorm-nc	CT	1913	Parkway St.
Ark. State UCA Campus	Powerhouse-nc	CT	1913	Parkway St.
Ark. State UCA Campus	Training Sch-nc	CT	1907	Parkway St.
Brown, Dr. G. S.*	R-nc	CT	1904	1604 Caldwell
Brown, Dr. G. S.	R-nc	CT		

106

CLIENT	BLDG-PROJECT	ARCHITECT	DATE	ADDRESS
Cole & Co.	Store front-add	CT	1908	
Conway School Dist.	School-nc	CT		
Conway School Dist	School-add	CT		Prince St.
Conway Telephone Co.	Office-bldg-nc	CT	1911	Parkway St.
Donaghey, G. W.	Office-store-nc	CT	1904	Front & Oak
Faber, Hicks	R-nc	T&H	1919	
Farmers State Bank*	Bank-nc	T&H	1918	1001 Front St.
First Baptist Church*	Private-nc	CT	1909	S.W. Corner Davis & Robinson
Frauenthal, Joe	Out-bldg-nc	CT	1914	
Frauenthal, Joe*	R-nc	CT	1913	631 Western
Frauenthal, Joe	Store-alt	CT	1915	Front St.
Frauenthal & Schwartz	Mercantile bldg.-nc	S&G		
Grummer Hardware Co.	Store front-alt	CT	1913	Oak & Chestnut
Hendrix College*	Martin Hall-nc	TH	1918	Hendrix Campus
Hendrix College	Dorm-nc Galloway Hall	CT	1913	Hendrix Campus
Jones, J. F.	R-nc	T&H	1922	N. Clifton St.
Keiser, J. F.	R-nc	CT	1911	
Little, Col. J. E.	R-alt	CT	1911	
Oliver, R. B.	Hotel-nc	S&G		
Reynolds, T. H.*	R-nc	CT	1913	Hendrix Campus
Robins, R. W.	R-nc	CT	1926	
Smith, S. G.	R-alt	CT		
Smith, S. G.*	R-nc	T&H	1924	1837 Caldwell
Smith, S. G.	R-nc			
Smith, S. G.**	Theater-nc	S&G	1923	Front St.

GARLAND COUNTY

HOT SPRINGS

CLIENT	BLDG-PROJECT	ARCHITECT	DATE	ADDRESS
Alhambra Bath House	Bath House-nc	CT		214 Quachita
Beauchamp, W. O.	R-nc	CT		492 Prospect
Bledin Hotel	Hotel-nc	S&G		
Community Bank	Bank-alt	TS&G	1930	
Como Hotel	Hotel-add	TS	1910-1920	
Como Hotel	Hotel garage-nc	TS	1910-1920	
Duffie, S. M.	R-nc	CT		700 Prospect
Eckel, G. M.	R-alt	TS&G	1910-1911	732 Park
Fellheimer, H.	Garage-nc	TS&G	1928	
Fellheimer, H.	R-nc	S&G		640 Quapaw
Firestone Tire	Store-nc	TS&G	1930	301-305 Ouachita
Fordyce, S. W.*	R-nc	CT		746 Park
Fordyce, S. W.	R-nc	CT		
Fordyce, S. W.	R-nc	CT		
Hale Bath House	Bath House-alt	TS&G		
Head, Frank	R-alt	S&G		
Hemmingway, Lois	Bath House-add	S&G	1938	
Hotchkiss, Douglas	Apart-alt	TS&G	1935	
Hotel Moody	Hotel-nc	CT	1913	
Hot Springs School Board	School-add	Ts&G		
House of Good Shepherd	Dorm-nc	TS&G	1929	
Howe Hotel	Hotel-nc	S&G		
Howe Hotel	Hotel-nc	S&G		
Interstate Orphanage*	Orphanage-nc	TS&G	1928	339 Combs St.
Johnson, E. H.	Store Hotel	CT	1904	
Jones, H. A.	R-nc	S&G		
Leon Levi Hospital	Nurses Home-nc	S&G		
Little & Sumpter	Store-nc	CT	1904	620 Central
Lonsdale, J. G.	R-add	S&G	1920	
Majestic Hotel	Hotel-alt	TS&G	1934	101 Park
McGill, Rev. R. M.	Store-add/alt	CT		
Mendel, Hubert	Store-alt	TS&G	1937	
Mendel, Hubert	Store-alt	TS&G	1937	
Mooney, Smith & Wood	Store-nc	TS&G		

Fig. 131 Skatzenstein House, Pine Bluff

CLIENT	BLDG-PROJECT	ARCHITECT	DATE	ADDRESS
Orr, C. G.	Hotel-nc	TS&G		
Park Hotel*	Hotel-nc	TS&G	1930	210 Fountain
Presbyterian Church*	Church-nc	CT	1907	213 Whittington
Presbyterian Church	Church-nc	CT	1907	
Presbyterian Church	Church-add	S&G	1925	
Presbyterian Church	Church-alt	TS&G	1928	
Rector, H. M.	Bathhouse-nc	R&T	1895	
Riviera Hotel*	Comm-nc	TS&G	ca. 1930	719 Central
St. Joseph Inf.	Hosp.-nc	CT		
St. Luke's Episcopal*	Church-nc	T&H	1923	Spring at Cottage Streets
Shaw, Dr. J. B.	Comm.-nc	TS&G	1935	338-344 Central Ave.
Singer, Charles	R-nc	S&G	1937	
Smith & Annan	Comm-nc		1929	
Tombler, C. M.	Apt-nc	CT		
Tombler, C. M.	Apt-nc	CT		
Wade, King*	Office-nc	TS&G	1927	231 Central
Wade, King	Office-nc	TS&G	1927	231 Central
Waukesha Hotel	Hotel-nc	R&T	c.1894	504-510 Ouachita
Williams, Hamp	Comm-nc	S&G		
Williams, Mrs.	Garage-nc	TS&G	1929	
Williams, Mrs.	Garage-nc	TS&G	1929	

GREENE COUNTY

PARAGOULD

CLIENT	BLDG-PROJECT	ARCHITECT	DATE	ADDRESS
Block, J. D.	R-nc	CT	1907	
Block, J. D.	R-nc	CT	1907	
Masonic Temple	Lodge-nc	CT	1906	
Paragould Trust	Office-nc	CT	1900-1910	

CLIENT	BLDG-PROJECT	ARCHITECT	DATE	ADDRESS

HEMPSTEAD COUNTY

BLEVINS

Bank of Blevins	Bank-nc	CT	1912	

HOPE

Anderson, Roy	R-nc	T&H	1922	
Bridewell, W. F.	R-nc	CT	1912	
Foster, Charles	R-nc	CT		
Foster, W. Y.*	R-alt	CT		303 N. Hervey
Foster, W. Y.	R-alt	CT	1911	
Gillespie, R. R.	R-nc	CT		
Henry, J. R.	R-nc	CT		
McRae, Dorsey*	R-nc	CT		1113 E. Third
Reed, S. L.	R-nc	CT		
St. Mark's Church**	Church-nc	CT	1904	Third & Elm Streets

HOT SPRING COUNTY

MALVERN

Anderson, J. A.	R-nc	CT	1921	
Ark. Land & Lumber	Store-nc	CT	1913	
Barlow, John D.	Hotel-alt	TS&G	1928	
Butler, D. C.	R-add/alt	CT		
Chamberlain, J. E.	R-alt	T&H	1920	
Chamberlain, J. E.	Store-alt	CT	1925	210 S. Main
Clark, D. D.*	R-nc	CT	1916	1324 So. Main
Farmers & Merchant	Bank-nc	CT	1913	
First Nat'l Bank	Bank-nc	CT		Main & Page
Hot Spring Co.	Courthouse-nc	TS&G	1935	Locust Street
McDonald, H. L.	R-nc	CT		Ash Street
McHenry, T. R.	Store-nc	CT		
McHenry, T. R.	Store-lodge	CT	1902	
Nunn, T. E.	Store-nc	CT	1925	321 Main Street
Rockport Lodge	Club-add	CT	1914	
Rockport Lodge	Club-add	TS&G	1930	
Strauss, A.*	R-nc	T&H	1919	528 E. Page
Strauss, A. L.	R-nc	CT		
Strauss, C. W.	R-nc	CT	1926	

INDEPENDENCE COUNTY

BATESVILLE

Adler, N. A.*	R-nc	TS		292 Boswell
Adler, N. A.	R-nc	CT		
Barnett, Charles	R-nc	CT	1916	
Batesville Bank	Bank-nc	R&T	c.1893	
Casey, S. M.	R-nc	CT	1915	551 Boswell
Crouch, A. L.	Store-nc	T&H	1919	
Dowdy, R. A.*	Store-nc	TS		154 South Third Street
Ferrell, J. W.	R-nc	CT		919 Main
Ferrell, J. W.	R-alt	CT		
Hanford, J. S.	R-alt	T&H	1917	909 Boswell
Jones. W. O.	R-nc	T&H		
Masonic Order	Orphanage-nc	CT	1907	
Masonic Order	Orphanage-alt	CT		
Masonic Temple	Temple-nc	R&T	c.1894	
Metcalf, C. D.	R-add	CT	1916	679 Boswell
Mitchell, W. A.*	R-nc	T&H	1917	1138 East Main
Odd Fellows	Orphanage-add	CT	1907	
Perrin, W. F.	R-nc	TS		476 Boswell
Presbyterian Congregation	Church-nc	TS		
St. Paul's Apostle*	Church-nc	CT	1916	Fifth & Main

Fig. 132 B.P.O.E., now Women's City Club, Little Rock

CLIENT	BLDG-PROJECT	ARCHITECT	DATE	ADDRESS

JACKSON COUNTY

NEWPORT

CLIENT	BLDG-PROJECT	ARCHITECT	DATE	ADDRESS
Billingsley, W. A.	Store-alt	CT		
Country Club	Club-nc	TS&G	1931	
Erwin, C. M.	R-nc	CT	1900-1910	
First Presbyterian Church*	Church-nc	S&G	1910-1920	4th & Main
Gregg, Tom*	R-nc	S&G	1920-1930	412 Pine
Hazel Hotel	Hotel-nc	TS&G	1930-1940	
Henry, Charles	R-nc	CT	1900-1910	
Hinkle, Roy	R-nc	S&G		Three Park Place
Jackson Co.	Courthouse-alt	CT	1900-1910	Third & Main
Jones, O. E.	Store-nc	S&G		
Martin, G. C.	R-nc	CT	1900-1910	
Martin, G. C.	R-nc	CT	1910-1920	
Midland Services	Gas Station-nc	S&G	1920-1930	
Newport School Board*	Sr. High-nc	TS&G	1930	Remmel Park
Newport School Board	Sr. High-nc	TS&G	1930	
Newport School Board	School-add	S&G		
St. Cecelia Chapel	Church-nc	TS&G	1930-1940	Main & Remmel St.
Sanders, H. C.	Store-alt	TS		
Watson, T. J.	Store-nc	CT	1910-1920	
Watson, T. J.	Store-nc	CT	1906	
Watson Estate	Store-nc	S&G	1927	
Wilderson, A. C.	Store-alt	TS&G	1929	308 Second Street
Wolff, Goldman Merchant	Store-alt	CT		Corner of Front & Hazel
Wolff, Goldman Merchant	Store-alt	CT	1902-1910	
Wolff, Goldman Merchant	Store-add	CT	1900-1910	
Wolff, Sigmund	Hotel-add/alt	CT	1900-1910	

TUPELO

CLIENT	BLDG-PROJECT	ARCHITECT	DATE	ADDRESS
Crittenden, Sharp	Store-nc	T&H	1918	

JEFFERSON COUNTY

ALTHEIMER

CLIENT	BLDG-PROJECT	ARCHITECT	DATE	ADDRESS
Bank of Altheimer	Bank-nc	CT		
Barnett, Mrs. R. B.	R-nc	T&H	1919	

FERDA

CLIENT	BLDG-PROJECT	ARCHITECT	DATE	ADDRESS
Van Etten Estates	Tenant homes-nc	T&H	1922	
Van Etten Estates	Farm manager house-nc	T&H	1922	

NEW GASCONY

CLIENT	BLDG-PROJECT	ARCHITECT	DATE	ADDRESS
Gracie, John M.*	R-nc	T&H		
Gracie, John M.	R-add	T&H		

PINE BLUFF

CLIENT	BLDG-PROJECT	ARCHITECT	DATE	ADDRESS
Altheimer, Ben	T-nc	CT		
Austin, Hon. M. A.*	R-add/alt	CT	1904	704 West Fifth
Austin, Hon. M. A.	Office & Store-nc	CT		
Austin & Head	Office & Store-alt	CT	1915	
Bridges, F. G.	R-nc	CT		
Bridges, F. G.	R-nc	CT		
Bridges, F. G.	Store-nc	CT	1914	S.W. corner of Main & Fifth
Collier, W. E.*	R-nc	CT	1913	1227 E. Fifth
Fox, H. C.*	R-nc	TS		1303 So. Olive
Freeman, E. W.	R-nc	G&S		
Graham & McKenzie	Store-nc	CT	1909	
G.U.O.O.F. Temple	Club-alt	T&H	1924	
Hammet Grocery Co.	Store-add	CT	1906	
Haizlip, Mrs. M.	R-nc	CT		
Hicks, Jeff; Senyard, Fred	Store-offices-nc	CT	1906	

CLIENT	BLDG-PROJECT	ARCHITECT	DATE	ADDRESS
Hosp. & Benevolent Assn.*	Davis Memorial Hosp.-nc	CT	1908	11th and Cherry
Hosp. & Benevolent Assn.	Davis Memorial	CT	1908	
Howson, L. G.	R(Garage)-nc	T&H	1918	1700 Olive
Howson, L. G.*	R-nc	T&H		
Hudson, J. H.*	R-nc	CT	1911	304 W. Fifteenth
Johnson, E. H.*	R-nc	CT	1912	315 Martin
Jordan, A. C.	R-nc	S&G		
Katzenstein, S.*	R-nc	CT	1913	902 W. Fifth
Merchants and Planters Bank**	Bank-nc	TH	1892	100 Main Street
Nichol, Mrs. Jo	R-nc	CT	1913	205 Park St.
Nunn, A. W.	R-nc	CT		
Pride, P. D.	R-nc	CT		
Puddephatt, Mr. William*	R-nc	CT		1820 So. Olive
Russell, S. B.*	R-nc	CT	1912	1617 S. Olive
Scull, F. Knox	Store-alt	CT	1909	
Scull, F. Knox	Store-nc	CT	1909	
Senyard, Fred	Store-nc	CT	1909	4th & Main Street
Senyard, Fred	R-add	CT	1912	617 Fifth
Senyard, Fred, & Bridges, F. A.	Store-alt	CT	1908	
Simmons Nat'l Bank	Bank-alt	CT	1916	
Temple, John	R-nc	S		1702 So. Oak
State Negro College	nc	TS&G	1928	Campus UAPB, Caldwell Hall

Fig. 133 S. H. Mann House, Forrest City

CLIENT	BLDG-PROJECT	ARCHITECT	DATE	ADDRESS

JOHNSON COUNTY

CLARKSVILLE

CLIENT	BLDG-PROJECT	ARCHITECT	DATE	ADDRESS
Arlington & Love Brothers	Garage-nc	T&H	1917	405 Main
Bank of Clarksville	Bank-alt	T&H	1919	
Davis, John M.	R-add/alt	CT	1907	
Davis, John M.*	R-nc	CT	1907	212 Fulton
Dunlap, D. Ward	Garage-alt	T&H	1917	
Dunlap, D. Ward*	R-nc	CT	1906	101 Grandview
Dunlap, R. D.	Livery Stable-nc	CT		
Hill Mercantile Co.	Store-alt	CT	1910	
May-Marlar Gro.	Warehouse-nc	T&H	1919	Taylor Street
McKennon, Dr. A. M.*	R-nc	CT	1907	115 Grandview Ave.
McKennon, Dr. A. M.	Store-nc	T&H	1917	403 Main
Ragon & Bowen	Livestock Room-nc	T&H	1918	North Fulton Street

SCRANTON

CLIENT	BLDG-PROJECT	ARCHITECT	DATE	ADDRESS
Scranton Bank	Bank-nc	CT		

LAWRENCE COUNTY

PORTIA

CLIENT	BLDG-PROJECT	ARCHITECT	DATE	ADDRESS
Tucker, F. W.	Store-nc	CT	1907	

WALNUT RIDGE

CLIENT	BLDG-PROJECT	ARCHITECT	DATE	ADDRESS
Dowell, S. C.	R-nc	CT		
Gibson, L. M.	R-nc	T&H	1918	
Gibson, L. M.	R-nc	T&H	1921	
Lawrence County	Courthouse-nc	CT	1900	
Lawrence County	Bank-nc	CT		
Walnut Ridge	School-nc	CT	1912	

110

Fig. 134 Roselawn Memorial Park office building, Little Rock

CLIENT	BLDG-PROJECT	ARCHITECT	DATE	ADDRESS
Walnut Ridge	School-nc	CT	1912	
Walnut Ridge	School-nc	CT	1906	

LEE COUNTY

MARIANNA

CLIENT	BLDG-PROJECT	ARCHITECT	DATE	ADDRESS
McClintock, J. M.**	R-nc	CT	1911	82 West Main
McClintock, J. M.*	R-nc	CT		43 Magnolia

LONOKE COUNTY

CARLISLE

CLIENT	BLDG-PROJECT	ARCHITECT	DATE	ADDRESS
Bank of Carlisle	Bank & Masonic Bldg.	CT	1907	

ENGLAND

CLIENT	BLDG-PROJECT	ARCHITECT	DATE	ADDRESS
Beakley, Mr. N. B.	R-nc	CT	1902	
Bank of England	Bank-nc	S&G	1930-1940	Main and England
Daughtry, R. S.	Store-nc	CT	1909	
Eagle, R.E.L.	R-nc	CT	1908	
England Nat'l Bank	Bank-alt	CT	1916	
England School Board	High school-nc	CT	1907	
Geyer & Adams Co.	Warehouse-nc	CT	1923	
Kennedy, W. S.	Comm-nc	S&G	1938	Haywood & Allis
Merchants & Planters Bank	Bank-nc	CT	1900-1910	
Schwartz, Mrs. L. E.	R-nc	T&H	1917	

KEO

CLIENT	BLDG-PROJECT	ARCHITECT	DATE	ADDRESS
Bowers, Dr. A. L.	R-nc	CT	1916	

LONOKE

CLIENT	BLDG-PROJECT	ARCHITECT	DATE	ADDRESS
Bell, J. A.	Lonoke City Bank-nc	CT	1906-1907	
Bransford, William	R-nc	S&G	1920-1930	
Cunning, Dr. John	Store-nc	CT		
Eagle, J. P. & Boone	Store & Office-nc	CT	1905	Front Street
Eagle, J. P. & Boone	Store-Office-nc	CT	1905	
Eagle, Joe P.*	R-nc	CT		217 Ash
Eagle, Joe P.	Store-nc	CT	1929	
Glover, S. S.	Store-nc	CT	1900-1910	
Goodwin, J. C., Sr.	Store-nc	CT	1900-1910	
Lonoke City Bank				
Rubel, A.	R-nc	CT	1900-1910	
Schull, O. L.*	R-nc	T&H	1917	418 Park
Trimble, T. C.*	R-nc	CT	1916	518 Center
Walls, Charles*	R-nc	CT	1913	406 Jefferson
Wheat, Pat H.	Store-nc	T&H	1920-1930	
Wheat, P. H.*	R-nc	CT	1900-1910	600 Center
Williams, R. L.	R-nc	TS		

SCOTT

CLIENT	BLDG-PROJECT	ARCHITECT	DATE	ADDRESS
Costin, B. R.	R-nc	CT		
Dortch, William P.**	R-nc	CT	1904	Marlsgate
Eyrie, All Souls Church**	Church-nc	CT		
Eyrie, All Souls Church	Church-add	T&H	1927	
Eyrie, All Souls Church	Rec hall-nc	CT	1900	
Eyrie, All Souls Church	Church	TS&G	1906	
Faver, E. M.	R-nc	CT	1927	
Galloway, D.F.S.	R-nc	T&H	1923	
Scott School District	School bldg.-nc	CT	1900-1910	

ASHVALE

CLIENT	BLDG-PROJECT	ARCHITECT	DATE	ADDRESS
Pemberton, J. M.	R-add	CT		

CLIENT	BLDG-PROJECT	ARCHITECT	DATE	ADDRESS

LOGAN COUNTY

MAGAZINE

CLIENT	BLDG-PROJECT	ARCHITECT	DATE	ADDRESS
Ouachita College*	Academy bldg.-nc	CT	1900	

PARIS

First National Bank	Bank-alt	S&G		Corner of Elm & Main

SCRANTON

Scranton Bank	Bank-nc	CT		

MILLER COUNTY

TEXARKANA

Dale, John (Arkadelphia)	Dale bldg.-nc	CT	1901	210 E. Third
Dean, Thomas M.**	R-nc	CT	1911	1520 Beach
Kittrell, Dr. T. P.*	R-nc	CT	1900-1910	1103 Hickory
Methodist Episcopal Church*	Church-nc	CT	1900-1910	6th and Laurel

MISSISSIPPI COUNTY

BLYTHEVILLE

Ingram, H. B.	Stores & Offices-nc	CT		

MONROE COUNTY

BISCOE

Fredonia Special School Dist.	School-nc	S&G		
Fredonia Special School Dist.	School-nc	S&G		

BRINKLEY

Brinkley School Board	High school-nc	CT		
Coca-Cola Bottling Co.	Comm-alt	S&G	1939	Main Street
First Methodist Episcopal Church	Sun. school-nc	CT	1926	
Folson, W. B.	R-nc	CT		Corner of S. Main & W. Elm
Gazzola & Vaccaro*	Store-office-nc	CT	1916	131-133 Cypress
Hale, M. E. (Mrs.)	R-nc	CT		
LoBelle, C. B.*	R-nc	CT		312 New York Avenue

CLARENDON

County Courthouse**	nc	CT	1911	
BPO Elks (1256)	Private-nc	TS		
CEL & P. Co. & Moore & Bateman	Comm-nc	CT	1913	241 Madison
Ike Bond	R-alt	TS		305 Jefferson
Merchants and Planters Bank*	nc	T&H	1921	214 Madison

HOLLY GROVE

Abramson, Mr. R.	R-nc	TS		
Mayo & Mayo	Store-nc	TS		

MONTGOMERY COUNTY

MT. IDA

Mt. Ida School Board	School-nc	TS		

NEVADA COUNTY

PRESCOTT

Bank of Prescott	Bank-nc	CT	1912	E. Elm & E. Second
Bank of Prescott	Bank-alt	CT	1914	E. Elm & E. Second
Bank of Prescott	Bank-add/alt	CT	1927	E. Elm & E. Second
Bemis, Ethel	T-nc	TS&G	1935	118 E. Elm
Bemis, Miss Norvelle	Florist-nc	CT		117 E. Second
Cox, E. L.	R-nc	S&G		
Gutherie, Martin	R-nc	T&H	1922	224 E. Ross
Hamby, Hon C. C.	R-nc	CT		924 Ash
Hamilton, H. A.	Store-alt	CT	1910	W. Main & W. First
Hesterly, Dr. S. J.	R-nc	CT		
McKenzie, H. B.	R-nc	T&H		302 Main
McRae, D. L.*	R-nc	CT		424 E. Main
McRae, Hon. T. C.	Ozan Merc Co-nc	CT		
McRae, Hon. T. C.	Store-add	CT		120 E. Elm
McRae, Hon. T. C.	Store-nc	CT		216 E. Second
McRae, Hon. T. C.	Store & Office-nc	T&H		
McRae, Hon. T. C.	Store-alt	CT	1914	
McRae, Hon. T. C.	Store-add	CT	1914	120 E. Elm
McRae, Hon. T. C.	Store-alt	T&H	1918	
McRae, Hon. T. C.	Ozan Merc. Co-nc	T&H	1923	210-212 E. Second
McRae, Hon. T. C.	Warehouse-nc	CT		
McRae, Hon. T. C.	R-add/alt	CT		
McRae, T. C. Jr.*	R-nc	T&H	1919	506 E. Elm
Milburn, John M.	Store-nc	CT		
Nelson, N. B.	R-nc	T&H	1919	412 E. Second
Nevada Co.	Courthouse-nc	TS		
Presbyterian Congregation	Church-nc	CT	1911	
Presbyterian Congregation	Church-add/alt	CT	1927	
Presbyterian Congregation	Church-add/alt	CT	1927	
Presbyterian Congregation	Church-heating	CT		
Prescott Hardware	Store-nc	S&G		106 E. Elm
Prescott Hotel	Hotel-nc	CT		
Prescott School Board	School	G&S		

Fig. 135 Dr. A. M. McKennon House, Clarksville

CLIENT	BLDG-PROJECT	ARCHITECT	DATE	ADDRESS

OUACHITA COUNTY

CAMDEN

CLIENT	BLDG-PROJECT	ARCHITECT	DATE	ADDRESS
Brown, Walter W.	R-add/alt	CT		
Brown, Walter W.	R-add/alt	CT		
Camden School Board	School-nc	TS		
Congregation Beth El	Church-nc	S&G	1938	
Felsenthal, Miss Nora	R-add	S&G		
Morgan, A. L.	Store-nc	CT	1899	
Morgan, J. H.	R-add/alt	CT	1901	116-120 Washington
Morgan, J. H.	R-add/alt	CT		
Ouachita Co.	Courthouse-add	T&H	1923	
Ramsey, W. K.	R-nc	CT	1904	Cleveland & Graham St.

STEPHENS

City of Stephens	City Hall-nc			116 Ruby

PERRY COUNTY

PERRYVILLE

Perry County Girls' Camp	Great Hall	TS&G	1936	

PHILLIPS COUNTY

HELENA

Arkansas Utilities Co.	Comm-nc	TS&G	1933	
Arkansas Utilities Co.	Comm-nc	TS&G	1933	
Helena School District	School-nc	TS&G	1931	Beech & Elm
Horner, E. C.	R-nc	R&T	c.1892	
Hornor, J. S.	R-nc	CT		Porter & Beech
Owen, C. D.	R-nc	R&T	c.1893	
Phillips National Bank	Bank-nc	TS&G		
Phillips National Bank	Bank-nc	TS&G	1937	Righton & Cherry
Ready, E. S.**	R-nc	CT	1910	929 Beech Street
Tanner, A. N.	R-nc	CT		
Thompson, J. H.	R-nc	B&T		
Updegraff, G. T.	R-nc	CT		
West Helena Water Works	Comm-nc	TS&G	1933	
White, Willeford*	R-nc	CT		1015 Perry
Wilkes, L. J.	R-nc	R&T	c.1893	
Wooten, C. A.	R-nc	CT		

POINSETT COUNTY

WEINER

St. Anthony's Parish	Church-nc	TS&G		

POPE COUNTY

RUSSELLVILLE

Brown & Perriman	Store-nc	CT		
Russellville School Board	School-nc	CT	1907	
Swain, J. A.	R-nc	T&H	1921	713 W. Main

PRAIRIE COUNTY

BISCOE

Special School District, Fredonia	School-nc	S&G		

DES ARC

Bethel, H. B.*	R-nc	CT	1918	Erwin & Second
Edmonson, G. W.	R-nc	CT		

112

Fig. 136 Conway Library, Morrilton

CLIENT	BLDG-PROJECT	ARCHITECT	DATE	ADDRESS
Prairie County	Courthouse-add/alt	CT	1904	Second Street
Prairie County**	Courthouse-nc	CT	1913	
Lankford, Eugene	Store-nc	CT	1912	
Lankford, Eugene	Store-nc	CT	1913	Highway 70

HAZEN

Shields, W. C.	Hotel-nc	CT		
Simms, J. H.	R-nc	CT		

PULASKI COUNTY

GALLOWAY

Galloway, D.F.S.	R-nc	TH	1923	
Schaer, Fred	R-alt/add	CT		

LITTLE ROCK

Abeles, Estate, C. T.	Comm-nc	TS&G	1936	
Akin, C. B.	R-alt	TS&G	1934	
A.A.O.M.N.S.*	Al Amin Temple-nc	CT	1912	2100 Main Street
A.A.O.M.N.S.	Al Amin Temple-alt	CT	1911	2100 Main Street
Alexander, Mrs. Bettie	R-alt	T&H	1918	
Alexander, Mrs. L. J.	nc	CT		
Alexander, L. J.	Laundry-alt	S&G	1939	1000 W. Markham
Allen, Edward Wiley	R-nc	TS&G	1931	
Allsopp, Fred M.	Fredrika Hotel-nc	TS	1910	
Allsopp, F. W.	R-alt/alt	TS&G	1929	
Altman, L. H.	R-nc	T&H	1918	
Anderson, J. A.	R-nc	T&H	1918	
Anderson, J. W.	R-alt-Add	T&H	1915	2324 Ringo

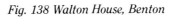

Fig. 137 Charles B. Foster House, Hope

Fig. 138 Walton House, Benton

CLIENT	BLDG-PROJECT	ARCHITECT	DATE	ADDRESS
Anderson, V. C.	R-nc	TS&G	1936	
Apple, Dr. W. J.		S&G	1938	2514 N. Fillmore
Arkansas Carpet & Furniture	Warehouse-nc	CT		
Arkansas Central Power	Store-nc	S&G		
Arkansas Democrat	Office-alt	TS&G	1930	E. Capitol & Scott
Archer, Mrs. E. M.	R-alt/add			
Armingway, Mrs. Lois K.	Store-alt	TS&G	1936	
Arnold, A.	Store-alt		1910	513 Center Street
Ashby, L. J.	R-nc	T&H	1917	416 W. 25th
Assn. Ref. Presbyterian Church*	Church-nc	CT		3323 W. 12th
Atenenbaum, Mrs.	Warehouse-nc	TS		
Back, J. D.	R-nc	CT		
Back, J. D.*	R-nc	CT	1905	1523 Cumberland
Back, William	R-alt	CT		
Baer, L. J.*	R-nc	CT	1915	1010 Rock
Baldwin, Mrs. Warren	R-nc	TS		2426 Louisiana
Bale, Hardin	Auto Shop-nc	S&G	1920	120 S. Broadway
Bankers Trust Co.	Office-add	CT	1915	
Bankers Trust	Office-nc	CT	1913	200 Main
Bathhurst, William R.	R-alt/add	T&H	1920	24th & Broadway
Batson, Rivers D.	R-nc	T&H		
Beal-Burrow Dry Goods	Office-alt	T&H	1920	
Bechle, G.**	R-nc	CT	1910	1000 E. Ninth Street
Bellingrath, T. L.	R-add	TS&G	1936	1820 Beechwood
Bentley, Dr. C.E.	R-nc	S&G	1917	1200 McAlmont
Beyerlein, Alice*	R-nc	CT	1916	412 W. Fourteenth
Biddle, Bruce	R-alt	TS&G	1934	1867 Gaines
Billingsley, C. A.	R-nc	CT	1907	2501 Izard
Billingsley, C. A.	R-nc	CT		

CLIENT	BLDG-PROJECT	ARCHITECT	DATE	ADDRESS
Bland, T. & Healy, W. B.	R-nc	T&H	1923	
Blass, Gus	Stable	CT		
Blass, Gus	Store-alt	TS&G		
Blass, Gus	Warehouse-nc	CT		
Blass, Jacob	Comm-nc	CT	1911	
Blass, L.	R-alt/add	CT		
Blass, Noland	R-alt	T&H	1922	1900 Summit
Bloom, Mrs. Annie	R-nc	TS		102 Berry
Bodeman, B.	R-nc	CT		
Bogen, S. Ellen	R-nc	CT		
Bona, James	Store-nc	S&G	1920	Tenth & High Streets
Bond, Mrs. W. C.	R-nc	T&H	1918	
Booker, Roberts M.	R-nc	CT		
Booker, Mrs. W. H.	R-alt	CT		
Bookman, B.	R-nc	CT	1907	
Boone, Dan M.*	R-nc	T&H	1927	4014 S. Lookout
Bottorff, K.	R-nc	CT		
Boyle Realty Co.	Store-nc	S&G		
Boyle Realty Co.	Comm-nc	S&G	1922	500 S. Main
Boyle Realty Co.	Comm-nc	TS&G	1930	
Boyle, J. F.	Comm-nc	S&G		311-317 W. Capitol (5th & Broadway)
Boyle, F. J.	R-add	CT		
Boyle, Lou Refining Co.	Filling Station-nc	TS&G	1935	8th & Broadway
Brack, G. S.	R-nc	CT		
Brack, Mrs. Vivian	R-nc	CT	1910	
Bracy, Eugene	R-nc	CT		
Bradschaw, D. E.	R-nc	CT		
Bragg, C. E.	R-nc	CT		
Bragg, F. C.	R-nc	T&H	1918	2704 Gaines Street

CLIENT	BLDG-PROJECT	ARCHITECT	DATE	ADDRESS
Brien, E. O.	R-nc	CT		
Brinkley Hospital	add	S&G	1939	
Brizzolara, A. B.	Store-nc	CT		
Brizzolara, A. B.	Stable-nc	CT	1916	
Brooks, S. M.	R-nc	S&G		464 Ridgeway
Brooks, M. W.	R-nc	TS	1917	1869 Izard
Brown, George R.	R-alt	R&T		
Brown, Oglesby Co.	Warehouse-nc	T&H	1920	
Browning, Mrs. B. R.	R-nc	CT	1913	
Bruce, E. L.	R-nc	S&G		Van Buren & N. Lookout
Buchanan, E. C.	R-nc	CT		
Burger, J.	R-nc	T&H	1925	818 Scott
Burns, J. W. of Mexico City	R-nc	CT		
Burr, A. H.	R-nc	T&H		
Bush, A. E.*	R-nc	T&H		1516 Ringo
Butler, C. M.	Store-nc	CT		
Butler, R. Colburn	R-nc	CT	1910	1408 Battery
Butterworth, A. C.	R-nc	CT	1915	
Calvary Cemetery	Entrance Gate-nc	TS&G		
Campbell, C. B.	R-alt	T&H	1924	2814 Gaines
Cantrell, D. H.	R-alt	T&H	1922	
Cantrell, D. H.	R-alt	CT	1911	
Cantrell, D. H.	R-alt	CT	1913	
Cantrell, D. H.	Apts-nc	CT	1910	
Cantrell, D. H.	Store-alt	CT	1910	
Capitol Furniture Co.	Factory-nc	CT		
Capitol Realty Co.	nc	S&G		
Capitol Realty Co.	nc	S&G		
Carmon, Mary	R-nc	CT		
Carnall, Mrs. Rachel	R-nc	CT		
Carter, Hugh	R-nc	T&H	1917	
Caruth, Luther	R-alt	TS&G	1934	903 Pulaski
Central Presbyterian Church*	Social Rm-nc	T&H	1921	1921 Arch
Chamber of Commerce	office-bldg.-alt	CT	1916	
Chamber of Commerce	office-bldg.-alt	CT	1911	
Chenault, Fletcher	R-nc	S&G	1922	2701 Izard
Cherry, C. W.	R-nc	CT		
Cherry, Mrs. L. W.	R-alt	TS&G	1928	700 Rock
City Delivery Co.	Icehouse-nc	S&G		
City of Little Rock**	City Hall-nc	CT	1906	500 West Markham
City of Little Rock	Hospital-nc	CT	1918	11th & McAlmont
City of Little Rock	School	CT	1907	
City of Little Rock**	Fire Dept. Hq-nc	CT	1912	N.E. Corner Markham & Arch
City of Little Rock	Library-add	TS&G	1937	700 Louisiana
City of Little Rock	Electric Power Plant	TS		
City of Little Rock	Power House	TS	1910	
Clark, C. W.	R-nc	CT		
Clark, George W.	R-nc	CT		
Clary, J. C.	R-nc	TS		
Coate, George E.	R-nc	T&H	1920	
Coca-Cola Co.	Bottling plant-alt	TS&G	1930	
Coca-Cola Co.	Industrial-alt	S&G	1939	515-525 W. Capitol
Coffman, C. T.	R-nc	CT	1911	
Coffin, Maxwell	R-nc	CT		
Cohen, A. K.	R-nc	TS		
Cohn, Mrs. A. D.	R-add	S&G		203 North Woodrow
Cohn, Morris M.				
Cole & Company	Comm-add	CT	1908	
Coleman, Mrs. C. T.	Comm-alt	TS&G	1934	
Colonial Development Co.	R-nc	S&G		
Colonial Development Co.	R-nc	S&G		
Coliseum Roller Rink	Rink-add	CT		
Collamore, L.	R-nc	CT		
Concordia Assn.	Club-add	S&G		
Cone, Mrs. J.	R-nc	CT		

CLIENT	BLDG-PROJECT	ARCHITECT	DATE	ADDRESS
Confederate Home	Hospital-add	T&H	1923	
Continental Banking Co.	Bank-nc	T&H		1324 Main Street
Cook, M.D.L.	R-nc	TS		
Cornish, Ed*	R-nc	TS	1917	1800 Arch
CRI & P Railroad	Pulaski Heights Sts.-nc	CT	1909	
Crawford, D. (Agent)	Store-Office-nc	CT	1909	
Crawford, T. D.	R-nc	CT	1919	416 Fairfax Avenue
Christ Church	Parish House-nc	TS&G	1928	501 Scott
Crittendon Home, Florence*	nc	T&H	1917	11th & Valentine
Croxon, Forrest N.*	R-nc	CT	1908	1901 Gaines
Culpepper, J. E.	R-nc	S&G		
Cuneo, Mrs. J. B.	R-nc	TS&H	1914	
Daniels, T. L.	R-nc	T&H	1919	
Darragh, Kramer*	R-nc	CT	1915	2412 Broadway
Dashiell, Bob	R-nc	CT	1907	1320 Schiller
Davis, Gov. Jeff	Barn-nc			
Davis, Kate L.	R-nc	CT		
Davis, S. P.	R-add/alt	T&H	1922	523 E. Capitol
DeBardeleben, J. M.	R-nc	S&G		
DeJarnett, P. L.	Store-nc	CT	1909	2401 Wright
Democrat Printing & Lithograph Co.	Office-nc	S&G		Second & Scott
Denison, George	R-nc	CT		
Denison, George	R-nc	CT	1916	
Dibrell, Melson & Handling, Drs.	Comm-nc	TS&G	1938	
Dickinson Hardware	Store-nc	CT	1893	
Dickinson, Horace of Canton, China	R-nc	CT	1912	
Dillion, E. B.	Apts.-nc	T&H	1924	
Donaghey, G. W.	Comm-nc	CT	1906-1911	7th & Main, S.E. Corner
Donham, Judge W. R.	Riviera Apts.-nc	TS&G	1928	
Donahoe, Mrs. Mary	R-nc	CT	1901	
Dooley, P. C.	R-nc	FR		1208 Louisiana Street
Dortch, Mrs. W. P.	Stores-nc	CT	1913	
Doyle, Mrs. T. N.	R-alt	T&H	1917	
Doyle Dry Goods	Store-nc	T&H	1923	
Doyle-Kidd Dry Goods	Store-nc	T&H	1921	
Dunaway, M. E.*	R-nc	CT	1915	2022 Battery
Dunn, M. E.	Store-nc	CT	1905	
Durst, Frank C.	R-nc	CT		
Durst, H. A.	R-nc	CT		
Durst, H. A.	R-nc	CT		
Durst, H. A.	R-nc			
Drees, Charles	R-nc	CT	1915	
Eichenbaum, E.	R-nc	TS		
Elkins, M. W.	Garage-nc	T&H	1922	2121 Gaines
Elks #29, B.P.O.*	Club-nc	TS	1908	401 Scott
Ellenbogen, S.	R-nc	CT		
Ellis, E. E.	R-nc	TS&G	1936	Shadowlane
England, Shelby*	R-nc	CT	1917	2121 Arch
English, E. Y.	R-nc	CT	1908	
Exchange National Bank	Bank-nc	T&H	1920	Main & Capitol
Falisi, Dr. J. V.	R-nc	CT	1913	
Farrell, R. E.	R-nc	CT	1915	
Farrell, R. E.	R-nc	CT	1914	2109 Louisiana
Farrell, R. E.	Garage-nc	CT	1914	
Farrell, R. E.*	R-nc	CT	1914	2111 Louisiana
Farrell, R. E.*	R-nc	CT	1914	2115 Louisiana
Farrell, R. E.*	R-nc	CT	1914	2121 Louisiana
Faulkner, A. M.	R-alt	TS&G	1934	5325 Lee Avenue
Faulhaber, C. E.	R-nc	CT	1906	
Federal Reserve Bank	Bank-nc	T&H	1920	123 W. Third
Fee, F. F.	Garage-nc	T&H	1921	
Field, E. J.	Apts-alt	TS&G	1937	

Fig. 139 Farmer State Bank, Conway

CLIENT	BLDG-PROJECT	ARCHITECT	DATE	ADDRESS
Fergurson, W. B.	R-nc	R&T	c.1892	
Finn, Lawrence	R-alt	TS&G	1934	
Firestone Tire Company	Service Bldg-nc	TS&G		
First M. E. Church	Church-nc	CT		
First Presbyterian Church	Sunday School-nc	CT	1913	Eighth & Scott, N.W. Corner
First Presbyterian Church	Church-nc	CT	1919	Eighth & Scott, N.W. Corner
First Church of Nazarene	Church-alt	CT		
Fletcher, Miss Alma*	R-nc	CT		909 Cumberland
Fletcher, Miss Alma	R-nc	CT	1907	E. Ninth & Cumberland
Fletcher, F. M.	R-nc	R&T	c.1893	
Fletcher, James	R-nc	CT		
Fletcher, James	R-nc	CT		
Fletcher, J. R.	R-nc	CT	1915	
Fletcher, Richard	R-nc	CT		623 Rock Street
Fletcher Coffee & Spice	Store-alt	CT		
Fletcher Coffee	Store-alt	CT	1913	409-411 E. Markham
Fones, J. R.	R-servant house-nc	CT		
Fones, J. R.	R-nc	CT		
Fones, J. R.	R-nc	CT	1912	
Fones Brothers Hardware	Shed-nc	TS&G	1929	
Fones, J. R.	Servant house-nc	TS&G	1930	
Fones, J. R.	R-nc	CT		
Fordyce, John R.**	R-nc	CT	1904	2115 Broadway
Fordyce, John R.	R-nc	CT		
Forney-Smith, Mrs. C. A.*	Apt-nc	CT	1914	1017 W. Fourth
Frank, Aaron	R-add	CT	1912	
Frauenthal, Hon. S.	Store-alt	CT		
Frauenthal, Charles*	R-nc	T&H	1919	2008 Arch
Frauenthal, Charles	R-nc	TS	1913	
French, F. L. & England, J. E., Drs.*	R-nc	CT	1900	1700 Broadway
Friederica Hotel	Hotel-alt	TS&G		600 Gaines
Froug, A.	R-nc	T&H	1919	1727 Center
Fuess, W. W.	Apts.-nc	S&G		483 Ridgeway
Fulk, Hon. F. G.	R-alt	T&H	1924	1910 Arch
Fulk Estate	Ark. Democrat Bldg-nc	CT	1916	613-615 Main
Fulk, F. G.	R-add	CT	1912	2001 Arch
Fulk, F. G.	R-nc	CT		2001 Arch
Funk, John	R-nc	CT		1923 Ringo
Gains, Jacot Estate of	Comm-nc	TS		
Galloway, D.F.S.	Store-nc	CT	1912	Sixth & Main
Galloway, D.F.S.	Store-nc	CT	1911	Sixth & Main
Gans, Sol & Gus; Leigh, L. B.	Store-nc	CT		
Gay, M. O.	Apt-nc	TS&G	1936	
Geige, Myrtle	R-alt	TS&G	1934	
General Hospital	Hospital-add	TS&G	1930	McAlmont & 12th
German Lutheran School	School-nc	CT	1907	East Eighth
Gersman, S.	R-nc	CT		
Geyer & Adams Co.	Warehouse-nc	CT	1914	405 E. Markham
Geyer & Adams Co.	Warehouse-alt	CT	1915	405 E. Markham
Gilmore, George W.	R-nc	S&G		604 Pine
Goldman, Lester	Comm-nc	TS&G	1928	
Goldman, Lester	Office-nc	CT		
Goldstein, Mrs. M.	R-nc	S&G		804 N. Ash
Goodnight, A. K.	R-nc	S&G		2120 Gaines
Goss, C. C.	R-alt	T&H	1919	
Goss, C. C.	R-nc	T&H		
Grain, Hayes	Industrial-nc	T&H		3900 Asher
Green, Mrs. M.	R-alt/add	CT	1911	
Greer, W. L.	R-nc	CT	1906	2113 Ringo
Griffith, C. J.	R-nc	S&G		
Grundfest, Dave	R-nc	TS&G	1937	
Gunnels-Riley Motor Co.	Office Bldg-alt	T&H	1918	

116

Fig. 140 Magnolia City Jail, Magnolia

CLIENT	BLDG-PROJECT	ARCHITECT	DATE	ADDRESS
Hall, W. G.	Store-nc	S&G		16th & High
Hall, Walter*	R-nc	TS&G	1928	32 Edgehill
Hall, W. G. Trustee	Store-nc	S&G	1921	Seventh & Spring
Hamberg, A. D.	Warehouse-nc	TS		
Hamberg, A. D.	Garage-nc	S&G	1926	Fourth & Cumberland
Hamilton, Errett	R-nc	CT	1911	
Hamlen, J. R.	R-nc		1914	
Hammons, G. C.	R-nc	TS		
Hardeman, W. O.	R-nc	CT	1908	
Hardy, M. W.	R-nc	T&H	1919	
Hardy, M. W.*	R-nc	T&H	1921	2400 Broadway
Hardy, M. W.	Garage-nc	T&H	1921	2400 Broadway
Harris, Dr. A. E.	R-nc	T&H	1917	
Harrod, J. H.	R-alt/add	CT		2000 Broadway
Hatfield, F. C.	R-nc	TS		321 Fairfax
Hayden, C. E.	R-nc	R&T	c.1892	
Hayes, Gaughy	R-nc	CT	1912	2420 Broadway
Healey & Roth*	Mortuary-nc	S&G	1925	815 Main
Healy, W. B. & Bland, T.	R-nc	T&H	1923	
Heibach, William	R-nc	CT	1907	1501 Summit
Heiman Estate	Comm-alt	CT	1911	
Hemingway, Lois Roots	Store-alt	TS&G	1936	
Hemingway, W. L., Agent	Store-nc	CT	1919	
Hemingway, Hon. W. E.*	R-nc	R&T	1895	1720 Arch
Herring, J. S.	Store-nc	CT	1910	
Himstedt, Henry	R-alt/add	CT		
Himstedt, Henry	R-nc	CT	1926	824 W. 25th
Holley, C. C.	R-nc	CT	1906	2101 Izard
Hornibrook, Jas. T.	Out-bldg.-alt	CT		
Hotze, Peter**	R-nc	CT	1905	1619 Louisiana

Fig. 141 Charles Fraunthal House, Little Rock

CLIENT	BLDG-PROJECT	ARCHITECT	DATE	ADDRESS
Houck, J. F.	R-nc	CT		
Hollis & Co.	Comm-alt	TS&G	1929	
Howland, Miss F. M.	R-nc	CT	1914	
Hundling, Dr. H. W.	R-nc	TS&G		
Hundling, Dr. H. W.	R-nc	TS&G	1935	
Hunter Memorial M. E. Church	Sunday School-nc	CT		712 E. 11th
Hurst, H. A.	R-nc	CT		
Imperial Laundry	Comm-nc	S&G		1501 Main
Irvine, E. D.	R-nc	CT	1900	2424 Gaines
Jackson, Vernon	R-alt/add	T&H	1922	1605 W. 24th
Jacksonville School District	School-add	CT		
Jacobson, J.	R-nc	CT		
Jansen, Mrs. P. J.	R-nc	CT		
J.C. Penney Company	Store-alt	TS&G	1937	
Jewish Cemetery	Chapel-mortuary & sexton lodge-nc	TS		
Jewish Synagogue	Synagogue-nc	R&T		
Johnson, A. W.	R-nc	CT		
Johnson, Col. B. S.	R-alt	CT	1905	507 E. Seventh
Johnson, Col. B. S.*	3R-nc	CT		514-518-516 E. Eighth
Johnson, T. T.	R-nc	CT	1910	409 E. 10th
Jones, D. W.	R-alt	R&T	1895	
Jones, E. S.	R-nc	CT		
Jones, J. R.	R-nc	CT		
Kahn, Gus	R-alt	T&H	1923	
Keatts, Jas. et al	Store-alt	CT	1916	104-106 Main
Keatts, Harry	R-nc	CT	1906	2216 Main
Keiser, J. F.	R-nc	CT		
Keith, A. M.*	R-nc	CT	1912	2200 Broadway

CLIENT	BLDG-PROJECT	ARCHITECT	DATE	ADDRESS
Keith, Alex M.	Duplex-nc	S&G		2016 State
Kelly, William	R-nc	CT	1915	
Kempner, Ike	"The Enid"-apt-nc	TS	1915	
Kempner, Ike	Stable-nc	CT		
Kilbury, M. J.	R-nc	S&G		
Kinsworthy, E. B.	Comm-alt	CT	1909	
Kirkwood, T. W.	R-nc	CT		
Kirkpatrick, Lemuel	6 Cottages-nc	CT		
Knights of Pythias	Castle Hall-alt	S&G		
Knights of Pythias	Castle Hall-nc	CT	1910	
Koen, W. O.	R-nc	T&H	1919	
Lady of Good Country Church	School-add	S&G		9th & Bishop
Lafferty, Thomas	Store-nc	CT		
Lafferty, Thomas	Store-nc	CT		
Lasher, Mrs. A.	R-nc	CT		
Lasker Brothers	Store-nc	S&G		
Lasker, M.	Comm-nc	S&G		
Lawrence, A. L.	R-nc	CT		
Ledbetter, C. R. & Associates	Warehouse-nc	T&H	1917	
Ledbetter, C. R.	R-alt	T&H	1917	
Ledbetter, C.	R-alt	S&G	1940-1941	4600 Crestwood
Ledbetter & Price	R-nc	CT		
Leigh	Comm-alt	CT	1911	
Leigh, L. B.	Office-nc	CT	1910	
Leigh, L. B. & Gans, S.	Comm-nc	CT		
Leiper & Mills, Messrs.	Store-nc	CT		
Lenon, W. E.	R-alt-add	CT	1916	2005 W. 16th
Lesser, Goldman	Office-nc	CT	1925	
Lesser, Goldman Cohen Co.	Comm-nc	CT	1925	
Lesser, Goldman	Comm-nc	TS&G	1928	
Levin, Barney	R-nc	CT		
Levinson, Henry	R-nc	S&G		
Levy, Laura	R-alt/add	CT	1911	
Levy, M.	R-nc	CT		
Lewis, Roy	R-alt	TS&G		
Leymer, Alfred	R-nc	CT		
Lincoln, C. J. Company	Drugstore-alt	CT		
Lincoln, C. K.	Store-nc	TS&G	1928	
Lipscombe, George A.	R-nc	CT	1911	
Lippingott, J. W.	Store-warehouse	CT	1905	
L.R. Athletic Assn	Club-add	S&G		
L.R. Boys Club*	Clubhouse-nc	TS&G-WD&W	1930	Eighth & Scott
L.R. Ref. & Elec. Co.	Comm-alt	CT	1915	
L.R. College	Gym-nc	CT		
L.R. College	Laundry-boiler-nc	CT	1911	
L.R. College	School-nc	CT	1911	
L.R. College	Fitzgerald Hall-nc	CT	1911	
L.R. Gas & Fuel Co.	Office-nc	CT	1925	
Little Rock School for the Blind	School-nc	BB	c.1885	Eighteenth and Center
L.R. School Board	Pulaski Heights Sch-add	TS&G	1935	
L.R. School Board	Forest Park Sch-nc	S&G	1923	Tyler & "P" Street
L.R. School Board	James Mitchell Sch.-nc	CT	1908	24th & Battery
L.R. School Board	James Mitchell Sch. add/alt	CT	1910	24th & Battery
L.R. School Board	Lincoln Sch-nc	CT	1907	
L.R. School Board	Pulaski Heights Jr. & Grammer Sch.-alt	T&H	1919	
L.R. School Board	Pulaski Heights Jr. & Grammer Sch.-alt	TS&G	1935	

CLIENT	BLDG-PROJECT	ARCHITECT	DATE	ADDRESS
L.R. School Board	Pulaski Heights Jr. & Grammer Sch.-alt-nc	T&H	1918	
L.R. School Board	Pulaski Heights Jr. & Grammer Sch.-alt	T&H	1919	
L.R. School Board	Pulaski Heights Jr. & Grammer Sch.-alt	TS&G	1929	
L.R. School Board	Pulaski Heights Jr. & Grammer Sch.-add/alt	TS&G		
L.R. School Board	Pulaski Heights Jr. & Grammer Sch.-add	TS&G	1934	
L.R. School Board	R.E. Lee Sch-add	TS	1910	
L.R. School Board	R.E. Lee Sch-add	TH	1930	
L.R. School Board	School-nc	CT		13th & State
L.R. School Board	Garland Sch-nc	S&G	1924	24th & Maple
L.R. School Board	Westside Jr. High-nc	TS	1917	14th & Marshall
L.R. School Board	Woodruff Sch-nc	TS	1915	7th & Booker
L.R. Zoo	Cat House-nc	TS&G	1934	Fair Park
Lloyd, J. T.	R-alt/add	T&H		
Lockhart, Maurice	R-alt	TS&G	1934	3322 W. 16th Street
Lofton, Lena	"Helena" Apts-nc	T&H	1917	
Lyon, W. O.	R-nc	S&G		
Lyons, G. H.	R-nc	CT		1520 Cumberland
McCabe, Mrs. M.D.	R-nc	CT		2113-2115 Arch
McCain, Mrs. W. S.	R-nc	CT		
McCarthy, James T.	R-nc	CT		
McClure, John	R-nc	CT		
McClurg, D. R.	R-nc	S&G		
McConnell, W. B.	R-nc	T&H	1925	
McCormick, B. W.	R-nc	TS		824 North Beech
McCook, S. D.	R-nc	S&G	1928	2215 Izard
McDairmid Bldg.	Office-nc	CT	1889	315½ W. Markham (East Pulaski Heights)
McDonald, J. S.	R-nc	TS		
McFarland, Milton	R-alt	TS&G	1936	224 N. Walnut
McGehee Hotel	Hotel-alt	TS&G		
McIlwain, W. J.	R-nc	CT	1903	2321 Gaines
McKesson-Lincoln Co.	Comm-alt	TS&G	1934	
McKinley, H. T.	Store-alt	T&H	1920	
McLean, A. E.	R-nc	T&H	1920	470 Ridgeway
McLean, A. E.				
Majestic Theatre	Theatre-nc	TS&G	1929	
Mahoney, J. J.	Hotel-nc	CT	1907	
Mahoney, Tom	R-nc	CT		
Malco Theatre	Theatre-nc	TS&G	1930	
Manufacturer's Furniture	Store-alt	TS&G	1936	
Marion Hotel	Hotel-alt	TS&G	1929	
Market Street Realty	Plunkett-Jarrell Gro-nc	CT	1905	
Marshall, J. C.*	R-nc	CT	1913	2009 Arch
Massar, A.	Comm-nc	S&G		
Masonic Lodge	add	CT	1911	
Masonic Lodge	add	CT	1911-1912	
Masonic Lodge	add	CT		
Masonic Lodge	add			
Massery, J. K.	Apt-nc	S&G	1938	706-708 Monroe
Mast, J. W.	Apt-nc	T&H	1920	1501-1507 Center
Matheny, Harriet C.	R-alt	TS&G	1934	5704 "R" Street
Mayer, Scott Company	Warehouse-nc	CT	1905	
Mayer, Scott Company	Warehouse-nc	CT	1914	808 E. Markham
Meek, Dr. E.	Store-nc	CT	1903	
Mehaffy, Hon. T. M.*	R-alt	CT	1911	2102 Louisiana
Mehaffey, Tom	R-add/alt	CT	1907	2102 Louisiana
Merchantile Trust Co.	R-nc	CT		
Mesler, H. S.	R-nc	CT	1913	
Moss, E. E.	Store-nc	CT	1915	
Methodist Church	nc	T&H	1921	1601 Louisiana
Metropolitan Hotel	Hotel-alt	CT	1909	
Metzger Estate	Comm-nc	TS&G	1934	
Miles, Hon. E. Company	Garage-nc	T&H		
Milliken and Kelly, Messrs.	Comm-alt	CT	1916	
Mitchell, Horace*	R-nc	CT	1911	1415 Spring
Mitchell, Mrs. W. S.	R-nc	CT		
Mitcham, Dr. Rease	Animal Hosp.-nc	TS&G	1936	
Montgomery, J. H.	R-alt	TS&G		
Moore, Hon. J. M.	Garage-nc	CT	1916	
Moore, Merrick*	R-nc	TS&G	1929	20 Armistead
Moore, John	Store-nc	T&H	1919	
Moore, M. B.	Store-nc	TS&G	1928	Sixth & Center
Morris, Emmett	R-nc	T&H		
Morris, Emmett	R-add/alt			
Morris, Rt. Rev. B.	Office-warehouse-nc	CT	1911	
Morrison, B.	R-nc	CT	1911	
Mt. Holly Cemetery*	Mausoleum-nc	T&H	1917	13th & Broadway
Murphy, Mrs. F. B.	Apt-nc	TS&G	1936	
Murray, E. C.	R-nc	CT	1910	804 W. 24th
Muswick, George	R-nc	CT	1907	
Mutual Real Estate Co.	Union Trust & Bank Bldg.	TS&G	1929	
Myers, Thomas T.	R-nc	CT	1912	812 N. Palm
Nash, Walter*	R-nc	CT	1907	601 Rock
Nash, Walter	R-nc	CT	1907	601 Rock
Nash, Walter*	R-nc	CT	1905	409 E. Sixth
Navra, Mrs. I.	R-nc	CT	1913	2101 Gaines
Neff, T. E.	R-nc	CT		1016 W. 21st
Niemeyer, George	R-nc	CT		1019 E. Ninth
Niemeyer, George	2 Cottages-nc	CT		
Niemeyer, Frank	R-nc	CT		
Niemeyer Lumber Co.	Store-nc	CT	1907	
Niemeyer, J. N.	R-nc	CT	1910	
Newton, C. M.	R-add/alt	CT		2008 Scott
Nichodemus, Charles	R-nc	TS&G		
Niemeyer, Jr.	Apts-nc	CT	1921	
Norton, S. A.	Apts-nc	CT	1916	2018 Louisiana
Oates Mattress Co.	Factory-nc	CT		
O'Brien, Jack	Store-nc	TS		
O'Brien, E.	R-nc	CT		
O'Brien, Ed	Comm-nc	S&G		
O'Leary, W.	R-nc	CT		
Oglesby, Brown	Warehouse-nc	T&H		
Oliver, E. S.	R-nc	CT		
Osborne, J. E.	R-add	CT		
Osborne, J. E.	R-nc	CT	1902	901 Welch
Page, Clyde	R-nc	CT	1910	
Park, C. E.	R-nc	CT	1914	
Parker, Mrs. C.	R-alt	TS		
Parks, Jessie & Connie	R-alt	TS&G	1934	2409 Howard
Paschal, Miss M. S.	Duplex-nc	CT	1911	
Pashley, Walter J.	R-nc	CT		
Pearson, R. M.	R-nc	S&G		
Pearson, R. M.**	R-nc	CT	1908	1900 Marshall
Peck, Sam Hotel	Hotel-nc	TS&G		
Peckham, H. A.	R-nc	CT		
Peckham, H. A.	R-nc	CT		
Peloubet, William C.	R-nc	TS		
Pemberton, S. M. K.	R-alt	TS&G	1934	2100 Ringo
Penick, James H.	R-nc	S&G		1623 Summit
Penzel Estate	Warehouse-nc	CT	1911	612 E. Markham
Penzel Grocery Co.	Warehouse-alt	T&H	1918	

Fig. 143 C. C. Reid House, Little Rock

120

CLIENT	BLDG-PROJECT	ARCHITECT	DATE	ADDRESS
People's Trust Co.	Comm-alt	TS&G	1929	
Peterson, William	R-nc	S&G		205 Ridgeway
Pfeifer Brothers	Clothing Store-alt	CT	1916	524 Main
Pfeifer Brothers	Store-nc	TS&G	1934	Sixth & Main
Pfeifer Brothers	Comm-alt	TS&G		514-524 Main
Pfeifer Brothers	Store-nc	S&G		
Pfeifer Brothers	Comm-alt	TS&G	1931	Sixth & Main
Pfeifer Brothers	Store-alt	TS&G		
Pfeifer Brothers	Store-nc	TS&G	1931	
Pfeifer, A. H.	R-nc	S&G		
Pfeifer, E. M.	R-nc	S&G		400 Fairfax
Pfeifer, Joseph Clothing Co.	Store-alt	CT	1912	
Pfeifer, Leo and Harry	Store-nc	CT	1909	
Pfeifer, Leo and Harry	Store-nc	CT	1906	
Pfeifer, Albert & Brothers	Store-nc	CT		
Pfeifer, Harry	R-add	TS&G	1937	
Pfeifer Brothers	Store-alt	T&H	1922	
Pfeifer, Louis	R-nc	CT	1906	523 W. Third
Pfeifer, Preston	R-alt & add	TS&G	1930	321 Fairfax
Pfeifer Estate	Warehouse-nc	CT		
Philander Smith College	Adm. Bldg-nc	TS&G	1930	13th & State
Philander Smith College	Girl's Dorm-nc	TS&G	1930	
Phillips, Arthur	R-nc	TS&G	1936	Ten Edgehill
Phillips, A. C.	R-nc	TS		
Phipps, Miss Minnie	R-add	CT	1912	415 E. Ninth
Pike, Albert Consistory	private-add/alt	CT	1911	Eighth & Scott
Pittsburg Plate Glass	Store-nc	TS&G		
Plunkett-Jarrell	Store-nc	CT		
Plunkett-Jarrell Grocery	Store-add/alt	T&H	1919	
Plunkett-Jarrell Grocery	Store-alt	CT	1914	

CLIENT	BLDG-PROJECT	ARCHITECT	DATE	ADDRESS
Plunkett-Jarrell Grocery	Store-vault	T&H	1918	
Plunkett-Jarrell Grocery	Store-wiring plans	CT	1914	
Plunkett-Jarrell Grocery	Store-alt	T&H	1920	
Poe, Tom	R-alt	TS&G	1935	1516 Broadway
Porter, Mrs. R. W.	Garage-nc	TS		
Porter, Lamar	Grandstand-nc	TS&G	1935	7th & Johnson, N.W. corner
Powell, C. W.	R-nc	CT		2223 Spring
Presbyterian Church, Second	nc	S&G	1924	
Price, C. G.	R-nc	CT	1911	
Price & Ledbetter	R-nc	CT		
Pulaski County	Garage-nc	T&H	1920	
Pulaski County	Detention-nc	CT	1925	
Pulaski County	Jail-nc	TS&G	1928	Broadway & Cantrell
Pulaski County School Board	School-nc	TS&G		
Purdon, Harry	R-nc	CT	1910	
Pythian Castle Hall	nc	CT		
Quapaw Investments	Office-nc	TS&G	1929	Fifth & Center
Ragland, William**	R-nc	R&T	c.1894	1617 Center
Ramey, H. M.	R-nc	G&S		
Read, A. C.	R-nc	TS		
Reaves, E. T.	R-nc	CT	1911	
Reeves, B. J.	R-alt	TS&G	1935	1904 Battery
Reichardt, Mrs. P.	R-alt	CT		1918 Welch
Reid, C. C.*	R-nc	CT	1911	1425 Kavanaugh
Reliable Furniture Co.	Store-alt	T&H	1920	
Remmel, H. L.*	Apt-nc	T&H	1917	
Remmel, H. L.*	Apt-nc	T&H	1917	411 W. 17th
Remmel, H. L.*	Apt-nc	T&H	1917	1708-1710 Spring
Remmel, H. L.*	Apt-nc	T&H	1917	1704-1706 Spring
Remmel, H. L.*	Apt-nc	CT	1906	1700-1702 Spring
Remmel, H. L.	R-alt	CT	1911	
Remmel, H. L.	Apt-alt	CT	1911	
Remmel, H. L.	Apt-alt	CT	1913	
Remmel, H. L.	Remmel Bldg-Office-nc	CT	1906	
Remmel, H. L.	Comm-alt	T&H	1920	
Remmel, H. L.	Store-nc	CT		
Remmel, H. L.	Store-nc	CT		
Remmel, H. L.	Store-nc	CT	1912	
Remmel, H. L.	Dye House-nc	CT	1909	
Retan, Mrs. A.*	R-nc	CT	1915	2510 Broadway
Reutlinger, J.	Store-nc	CT	1926	
Requa, T. P.	R-nc	CT	1901	
Rice, Mrs. P. J.	R-alt/add	CT		
Riegel, Emile	R-nc	CT		
Riffel, Kirby	R-nc	CT		
Robertson, T. N.	R-nc	CT		
Rogers, Dr. F. O.*	R-nc	CT	1914	400 W. 18th
Rogoski, A. V.	Store-nc	CT	1907	
Roots Estate	Occidental Bldg-alt	CT	1909	
Rose, Hon. U. M.	Comm-add	CT		
Roselawn Memorial Park*	Office-nc	T&H	1924	
Rosenbaum Machinery Co.	Office-nc	CT	1904	324 E. Second
Rottenberry, Burl C.	R-nc	T&H	1924	108 Thayer
Rowe, E. M.	R-nc	T&H	1919	
Royal Theater	Theater-nc	TS		400 Block of Main
Rudolph, Charles	Store-nc	CT		
Rudolph, Charles	R-nc	CT		
Rudolph, Charles	R-nc	CT		520 W. Sixth
Sanders, M. B.*	R-nc	TS	1917	2100 Gaines
Sanders, M. B.	Store-nc	TS		
Safferstone, T.*	R-nc	S&G		2205 Arch
Sanders, M. B.	R-nc	TS	1917	2100 Gaines
Sandlin, W. N.	R-nc	CT		2305 Gaines
Scarborough, Dr. James	R-alt	T&H	1919	1700 Arch
Schaad, Ben D. Machinery Co.	Warehouse-nc	T&H	1923	

CLIENT	BLDG-PROJECT	ARCHITECT	DATE	ADDRESS
Schaer, H. A. Jr.*	R-nc	T&H	1923	1862 Arch
Scheibner, Carl	R-alt	TS&G	1934	221 Rosetta
Schmuck, Henry	R-nc	CT		
Scoll, Sam	R-nc	CT	1913	2300 State
Scott, Dr. A. H.	Store-nc	CT		
Scott, Mrs. A. H.	R-alt	T&H	1917	1010 Louisiana
Scott, A. H. Estate	Comm-garage-nc	CT		
Scott, S. P.	R-nc	T&H	1921	323 Linwood Court
Scott, S. P. & Boyle, T.	R-nc	T&H	1922	
Scott, S. P., Jr.	R-nc	T&H	1923	
See, James P.	Apt-alt	CT	1916	
Seventh & Main Realty	nc	S&G		
Shall, Miss Lizzie	R-nc	CT		
Shanahan, Rev. P. J.	Parish house-nc	CT	1912	
Shannon, Tom	R-nc	CT		
Shelton, George	Garage-alt	T&H	1917	1803 Park Avenue
Shoemaker, Charles	Garage-nc	TS		
Shoemaker, B.	Comm-nc	S&G		
Shields, Mrs. Al	R-nc	CT		309 E. 15th
Simmons, G. S.	R-nc	S&G	1928	
Singleton, J. P.	R-alt	TS&G	1934	
Skillern, J. E.*	R-nc	CT	1915	2522 Arch
Skillern, J. E.	Stable-nc	CT		
Skillern, J. E.	Comm-nc	TS	1913	
Slaughter, D. P.	R-alt	T&H	1917	
Smith, Dr. Morgan	Apts-nc	CT	1914	2222 Louisiana
Smith, Dr. Morgan	Gas station-nc	T&H	1924	
Smith, Rudy	R-alt	T&H	1919	
Smith, W. B.	R-alt	T&H	1917	
Snyder, C. J.*	R-nc	S&G	1925	4004 Lookout
Solmson, Harry	R-nc	S&G		2000 Gaines
Solmson & Pfeifer	Store-nc	S&G		
Sowell, Mrs.	R-nc	CT	1907	
Spears, Will	R-alt	TS&G	1934	3419 Ringo
Spivey, H. S.	R-nc	CT	1907	2400 Gaines
St. Andrew Parish	Chap-nc	S&G		
St. Edward's Church**	Church-nc	CT	1901	823 Sherman
St. Mary's Academy	Main-bldg-add	T&H	1923	3224 Kavanaugh
St. Mary's Academy	Servants Qts-nc	CT		3224 Kavanaugh
St. Mary's Convent	Main bldg-alt	T&H	1920	3224 Kavanaugh
St. Mary's Convent & Academy	Auditorium-nc	T&H	1923	3224 Kavanaugh
St. Vincent's Infirmary	Hospital-alt	T&H	1917	
St. Vincent's Infirmary	Annex-add	CT		
St. Vincent's Infirmary	Nurses' Home-chapel-nc	S&G	1924	
St. Vincent's Infirmary	Private-alt	T&H	1917	
St. Vincent's Infirmary	Hospital-add	TS&G		
Stanton, William A.	R-nc	CT	1910	2121 Chester
Steiva, Dr. Elbert	3R-nc	TS&G	1935	Ninth & Scott
Stebbins, A. H.	R-nc	TS&G	1937	
Stewart, James M.	R-add/alt	CT		
Stewart, W. R.	R-nc	CT	1910	1406 Summit
Stainback, L. A.	R-alt/add	CT		
Stannus Estate	Store-alt	TS&G	1936	
State Hospital	Women's TB Ward-nc	T&H	1923	
State of Arkansas	nc	S&G		
Stainback, L. A.	R-alt/add	CT		
Steinbrenner, Sara	R-alt	TS&G	1934	
Steinert, R. C.	R-nc	CT		
Steiwell, Abe	Park Theatre-nc	TS		
Stewart, James M.	R-add/alt	CT		
Stewart, Dr. S. S.	Office-nc	CT		
Stewart, W. R.	R-nc	CT		
Stifft, Charles	R-nc	CT		
Stifft, Charles	R-add	CT	1912	
Sullivan, Walton Company	alt	TS&G	1912	
Sugrue, C. C.	R-nc	TS		
SWT&T Company	Office-alt	CT	1912	
Sugarman, V.	R-nc	TS	1914	
Taylor, Charles	Store-alt	TS&G		
Temple B'nai Israel	Synagogue-nc	R&T	1897	
Temple B'nai Israel	Synagogue-alt	CT	1912	
Temple B'nai Israel	Synagogue-alt	TS&G	1936	
Tennenbaum, A.	Comm-nc	S&G		
Terminal Hotel**	Hotel-nc	CT	1908	Victory & Markham
Thalman & Reed, Messrs.	R-nc	CT	1915	Cedar & 13th
Thomas, S. R.	Store-nc	T&H	1925	
Thomas, W. D.	Comm-nc	S&G		
Thomas, Hon. J. S.	R-nc	CT		
Thompson, Ada Home**	Home for Elderly-nc	S&G	1909	2021 South Main
Thompson, C.	R-alt	CT	1908	2114 Spring
Thompson, C.	R-alt/add	CT	1921	2015 Broadway
Thompson, George W.	Negro Lodge	R&T	1894	
Thompson, Richard	R-nc	CT	1914	2104 Battery
Thompson, Roy	R-nc	CT	1911	
Thompson, W. J.	R-nc	CT		
Thurston, Mr. Beverly*	R-nc	CT		923 Cumberland
Towey, John	R-nc	CT		
Treadway, W. A.	R-add	T&H	1922	2215 Louisiana
Trinity Hospital	Garage-nc	TS&G	1935	
Tuchfeld, Joel	Store-nc	CT		
Tucker, Henry	R-nc	T&H	1924	
Tucker, Jack	R-nc	TS&G		
Turner, Miss S. C.*	R-nc	CT	1906	1701 Center
U of A Medical School Board of Trustees	Folsom Clinic-nc	CT	1916	
Union Sunday School	Sunday School-nc	CT	1909	
Union Trust (Agents)	Ben D. Schaad Machinery Co-alt	CT	1916	
Union Trust Co. (Agents)	Store-alt	CT	1927	
Union Trust Co. (Agents)	Store-alt	CT	1911	
Union Trust Co.	Hunting Lodge-nc	CT	1914	
Union Trust Co.	Bank-nc	TS&G	1929	
Union Trust Co.	Comm-alt	T&H	1918-1919	
Union Trust Co.	Mortuary-nc	TS&G	1928	
Union Trust Co.	Bank-nc	TS&G	1929	
Union Trust Co.	Comm-nc	TS		Center & Capitol
Union Trust Co.	Comm-nc	CT	1914	
United Cigar Store Co.	Store-alt	CT		424 Main
Van Etten, Mrs.	R-nc	CT		
Van Etten, J. A.	Store-nc	CT		
Van Etten, A. E.	R-nc	CT		
Van Etten, A. E.*	R-nc	CT		1012 Cumberland
Vaughn, Mrs. M.*	R-nc	CT	1919	2201 Broadway
Vestal, Charles	R-add	CT		
Vinson, Baldy**	R-nc	CT	1905	2125 Broadway
Vinson & Read	Store & Apts-nc	CT	1911	
Vinson, J. R.	Store-alt	CT	1911	
Waldenberger, Joseph P.	R-nc	CT		
Walker, R. W.	R-alt	CT	1925	
Walton, Gus	R-nc	TS&G	1936	
Walton, Sullivan Co.	Comm-alt	TS&G		
War Memorial Building	Public-alt	TS&G		300 W. Markham
Ward, Sibley	R-nc	CT	1911	
Watkins, Mrs. C.	Apt-nc	CT	1909	
Watkins, Mrs. C.	R-alt	T&H	1917	
Weideman, Henry Jr.	R-nc	CT	1915	1871 Izard
Weinmann, John W.	R-alt	T&H	1921	9th & Cumberland
West, A. M.	R-nc	CT	1915	
West, S. Y.	R-nc	T&H	1918	

CLIENT	BLDG-PROJECT	ARCHITECT	DATE	ADDRESS
Whitcomb, J. A.	Store-alt	CT	1914	
Williams, D. E.	R-nc	T&H		
Williams, Hon. J. E.	R-nc	CT		1512 Gaines
Williams, Mrs. J. E.	Apt-alt	T&H	1923	1512 Gaines
Williams, Mrs. J. E.	R-alt	T&H		1512 Gaines
Williams, T. P.	R-nc	S&G	1939	
Williams, Robert	R-nc	CT	1913	
Williams, R. W.	R-nc	TS		
Williams, Robert	R-nc	CT	1913	
Wilson, A. J. Jr.	R-nc	CT	1907	
Wilson, Mrs. Nell	Apt-nc	TS&G	1935	
Wilson, G. W.	R-nc	CT		
Wilson, W. W.	R-nc	TS		
Woods, G. G.	R-add	CT	1916	
Woodsmall, S. Q.	R-nc	T&H	1922	
Worthen, W. B.	Stable-nc	CT		
Worthen, W. B. Co.	Comm-alt	TS&G	1936	
Wheatly, Phyllis YWCA			1919	
Winfield Methodist Church*	Church-nc	T&H	1925	1601 Louisiana
Yocum, Mrs. M. R.	R-add/alt	CT		1216 W. Second
YMCA Building	nc	FG	1900-1905	Sixth & Broadway

MARCHE

CLIENT	BLDG-PROJECT	ARCHITECT	DATE	ADDRESS
St. Mary's Immaculate Conception	Parish hall-nc	TS&G		
St. Mary's Immaculate Conception*	Church-nc	TS&G	1932	Blue Hill Road

NORTH LITTLE ROCK

CLIENT	BLDG-PROJECT	ARCHITECT	DATE	ADDRESS
Alexander, L. J.	R-nc	CT		
Argenta School Board	High school-nc	CT	1912	
Argenta, City of	Pump. plant-nc	CT		
Argenta Imp. Dist.	Pump. plant-nc	CT	1916	
Argenta, Bank of	Bank-nc	S&G		
Arkansas Natl. Guard	Caretakers Cottage-nc	TS&G	1931	
Arkansas Natl. Guard	Public-add	TS&G	1923	
Arkansas Natl. Guard	Admin. bldg-nc	S&G		
Arkansas Natl. Guard	Public-nc	S&G		
Arkansas Natl. Guard	Auditorium-nc	TS&G	1931	Camp Robinson
Arkansas Natl. Guard	Pavillion & pool-nc	TS&G	1931	Camp Robinson
Brod, John	R-nc	CT		
Brod, John	R-nc	CT		
Brod, John	R-nc	CT		
Messr. Cooper & Paine	Store-nc	CT		
Camp Pike	Officer's Mess-add/alt	TS&G	1930	
Camp Pike	NC	TS&G	1931	
City of N.L.R.	Fire dept-nc	TS&G	1937	
City of N.L.R.*	Post Office		1931	420 Main St.
Cook, M.D.L.	R-nc	TS		
Cuneo, Mrs. J. B.	R-nc	TS	1914	
Erion, J. P. & Ohal	R-add	TS&G	1934	
Faucette, J. P. & W. C.	R-nc	TS		320 W. Fourth
Faucette, J. P. & W. C.**	R-nc	TS	1912	316 W. Fourth
Faucette, J. P. & W. C.	R-nc	TS		
Garner, Mrs. M.	Comm-nc	S&G		
Goldberg, F. & I.	Store-nc	TS&G	1928	
Gibson, L. J.	R-nc	T&H	1924	Park Hill Addition
Haves Grain & Comm.	Warehouse-nc	T&H		
Herring, J. S.	Store-nc	CT	1907	
Hosack, Edwin & Maggie Ray	Res-alt	TS&G	1936	RR 3, Scenic Road
Howell, Dr. A. R.	R-nc	CT		300 W. Fourth Street
Howlard, John J.	R-nc	CT		
Improvement Dist #1	Public-nc	CT	1916	
Johnson, J. J.	R-alt	TS&G	1934	1218 Gillam Street

CLIENT	BLDG-PROJECT	ARCHITECT	DATE	ADDRESS
Johnson, Team & Dray	Comm-nc	S&G	1925	Under Broadway Bridge
Kahn, Adolf	R-nc	CT		
Kosciuszko Club	Clubhouse-nc	TS		
Lawhorn, Ross	R-add	TS&G		
Lewis, Roy	R-nc	TS&G	1934	1805 W. 16th Street
Machin, A. M.	R-nc	CT		
Malco Theaters	Theater-nc	TS&G	1930	
Meek, Dr. Edward	R-nc	CT		
Meek, Dr. Edward	R-nc	CT		
Merchants Transfer Co.	Comm-nc	TS&G		
Neale, J. E.	R-alt	TS&G		
Neely, Mrs. Tressie	R-alt	TS&G	1934	814 W. 24th Street
Presbyterian Church	add	T&H	1920	4th & Maple
Riegler, Fritz	R-nc	CT		
Runrill, Francis E.	R-alt	TS	1935	
State of Arkansas	Industrial-nc	TS&G	1931	
St. Mary's Parochial School	School-nc	S&G		
Seebacher, P.	R-alt	TS&G	1934	RR 4, Remount Road
Schneider the Tailor	Comm-alt	TS&G	1929	115 Main Street
Shipton, Georgia	Comm-nc	TS&G	1930	
Tannenbaum, A.	Comm-nc	S&G		109-111 E. Washington
Union Trust Co. (Agents)	Comm-alt	CT	1925	314-316 Main
Whitney, Harb, Inc.	Office-nc	TS&G	1930	
Williamson, R. W.	R-nc	TS		Midland Hills Addition

RANDOLPH COUNTY

MAYNARD

CLIENT	BLDG-PROJECT	ARCHITECT	DATE	ADDRESS
Ouachita Maynard Academy	School-nc	CT		

SALINE COUNTY

BAUXITE

CLIENT	BLDG-PROJECT	ARCHITECT	DATE	ADDRESS
Am. Bauxite Co.	Hospital-add	CT		
Am. Bauxite Co.	Theater-nc	T&H	1918	

Fig. 144 Old Central Fire Station, Little Rock

CLIENT	BLDG-PROJECT	ARCHITECT	DATE	ADDRESS
Gibbons, J. R.	R-nc	CT		
Pittsburg Reduction Co.	Office-nc	CT		

BENTON

CLIENT	BLDG-PROJECT	ARCHITECT	DATE	ADDRESS
Bell, J. K.	Store-alt	CT		102 South
Benton School Board	School-nc	CT	1905	
Coca-Cola Co.	Bottling Plant	TS&G		
First Nat'l. Bank	Bank-nc	CT		
Saline Co.**	Courthouse-nc	CT	1902	
Stinson, E. X.	Store-nc	CT		Sevier & Market
Womack, Charles	Store-nc	S&G		
Walton, Dr. James W.**	R-nc	CT	1903	301 W. Sevier

SEARCY COUNTY

LESLIE

CLIENT	BLDG-PROJECT	ARCHITECT	DATE	ADDRESS
Leslie School Board	School-nc	TS		

SEBASTIAN COUNTY

FORT SMITH

CLIENT	BLDG-PROJECT	ARCHITECT	DATE	ADDRESS
Christ the King Parish*	Church-nc	TS&G	1930	1920 Greenwood
Lincoln School	School-nc	R&T	c.1893	
Nowen, Charles D.	R-nc	CT	1895-1900	N. 16th & "D"
Waters, Pierce Oil Co.	Watershed-nc	CT		

ST. FRANCIS COUNTY

CALDWELL

CLIENT	BLDG-PROJECT	ARCHITECT	DATE	ADDRESS
Lanier, R. J.	R-nc	CT	1916	

FORREST CITY

CLIENT	BLDG-PROJECT	ARCHITECT	DATE	ADDRESS
Ash, E.	R-nc	TS&G	1932	
Bank of Eastern Arkansas	Bank-alt	CT	1916	Washington Street
Beck, J. W.	R-nc	CT		
City of Forrest City	City Hall-nc	S&G	1938	Rosser & Garland
City of Forrest City	Library	S&G	1938	Washington & Davis
Forrest City School	School-add	CT		
Gatling, John	R-nc	CT	1911	
Mann, J. M.*	R-nc	CT	1913	422 Forrest
St. Francis Co.	Courthouse-nc	CT		
St. Francis Parish	Church-nc	TS&G	1935	

HUGHES

CLIENT	BLDG-PROJECT	ARCHITECT	DATE	ADDRESS
Hughes School Board	School-nc	TH	1934	

WHEATLEY

CLIENT	BLDG-PROJECT	ARCHITECT	DATE	ADDRESS
Smith, H. K.*	R-nc	T&H	1919	Memphis Avenue

UNION COUNTY

EL DORADO

CLIENT	BLDG-PROJECT	ARCHITECT	DATE	ADDRESS
City of El Dorado	NC	TS		
El Dorado School Board	S. Side Grammar-nc	CT	1926	
El Dorado School Board	Grammar School-nc	CT	1928	Murphy, Wesson, Bullot, & Block
El Dorado School Board*	High School-nc	T&H	1924	Summit & Wesson
El Dorado School Board	High School-nc	T&H	1924	Wesson, Black, Summit
Garrett, R. N.	Barn-nc	TS	1906	
Garrett, R. N.	R-nc	TS	1906	
Garrett, R. N., Jr.	R-nc	TS&G	1937	1710 N. Madison
Goodwin, W. H.	Store-add	CT		
Horton, H. L.	R-nc	CT		504 N. Madison

Fig. 145 First Lutheran Church School, Little Rock

CLIENT	BLDG-PROJECT	ARCHITECT	DATE	ADDRESS
Leader Co.	Store-alt	T&H	1921	
Mahoney, Hon. E. O.	R-nc	CT	1908	
Meinert, R. E.	R-nc	S&G		711 Champinolle
Methodist Episcopal Church Soc.	Church-nc	CT		
Pinson, W. J.	R-nc	CT		
Sample Co.	McKinney Bldg-alt	T&H	1923	
Wilson, Mrs. A. G.	Store-nc	CT	1909	Jefferson & Elm
Wilson, Mrs. A. G.	Store-nc	CT		

WASHINGTON COUNTY

FAYETTEVILLE

CLIENT	BLDG-PROJECT	ARCHITECT	DATE	ADDRESS
Hemingway, W. E.**	Barn-nc	CT	1905-1907	3310 Old Missouri
Hemingway, Judge W. E.**	R-nc	CT	1905	3310 Old Missouri
Moore, Dr. A. A.	R-nc	CT		
University of Arkansas*	Dorm-nc	CT		Carnell Hall U of A Campus
University of Arkansas	Dorm-nc	CT		
Washington County**	Courthouse-nc	CT	1905	College Avenue & East Center
Waters Pierce Oil	Warehouse-nc	CT	1910-1920	

CLIENT	BLDG-PROJECT	ARCHITECT	DATE	ADDRESS

WHITE COUNTY

ARMSTRONG SPRINGS

CLIENT	BLDG-PROJECT	ARCHITECT	DATE	ADDRESS
Rev. Father Matthew OSB	Chapel-nc	TS&G	1928	
Morris Institute	Dorm & Class-nc	TS&G		

SEARCY

CLIENT	BLDG-PROJECT	ARCHITECT	DATE	ADDRESS
Blackburn, E.	R-alt	TS&G		500 W. Woodruff
Coca-Cola Co.	Bottling plant-add	TS&G	1937	
Deener, J. Hicks*	R-nc	CT	1912	310 E. Center
Galloway College	Gym-nc	CT	1920-1930	
Harding College	Dorm-nc	S&G	1920-1930	
Hicks, Ida	R-nc	CT	1900-1910	410 W. Arch
Lightle, Mrs. C. R.	Store-nc	TS&G	1929	
Lightle, J. E.	R-nc	R&T	c.1894	
Lightle, J. E.	R-nc	T&H	1929	
Lightle, Mrs. John*	R-nc	S&G	1923	605 Race
Lightle, W. H.	R-add/alt	CT	1890-1900	
Phoenix Club	Library-nc	TS&G	1930-1938	
Sanford, Mrs. S. W.	R-nc	CT	1913	410 W. Center
Searcy Male College	Adm-nc	R&T	1894	
Searcy Methodist	Church-add/alt	CT	1900-1916	304 Main
Skillern, J. E.	R-nc	R&T	c.1894	
Trinity Episcopal Church	Church-nc	CT	1895-1900	Elm & Arch, S.E. corner
Union Trust Co.	Bank-add/alt	CT	1910-1920	
Ward, R. A., Jr.	R-nc	T&H	1924	
Watkins, Tom A.				Race Street

WOODRUFF COUNTY

AUGUSTA

CLIENT	BLDG-PROJECT	ARCHITECT	DATE	ADDRESS
Augusta Merc. Co.	Comm-nc	S	1910-1920	117 S. Second
Augusta Merc. Co.	Warehouse-nc	CT	1900-1910	105 Front
Bank of Augusta	Bank-nc	CT	1920-1930	100 S. Second
Campbell, William	R-nc	CT	1919	500 N. Third
Cole, L. L.	Store-nc	T&H	1922	
Conner, Hon. E. H.	R-nc	CT	1904	305 S. Third
Conner, Hon. E. H.	Store-nc	CT	1895	111 N. Second
Conner, J. L.	R-nc	CT	1900	200 S. Fourth
Conner, J. L.	R-nc	CT		
Fitzhugh, R. K.	R-nc	CT		509 N. Third
Gardner, T. L.	R-nc	CT	1912	205 N. Third
Gregory, Nathan	R-nc	CT	1915	312 S. Second
Heckart, C. C.	R-nc	CT	1900-1910	826 N. Third
Methodist Episcopal Church Soc.	Church-nc	CT	1909	301 S. Third
Methodist Episcopal Church Soc.	Church-alt	T&H	1920	
Stacy, C. R.	R-nc	CT	1914	301 S. Fourth
Woodruff County*	Courthouse-nc	CT	1901	500 N. Third
Woodruff County	Jail-add	CT	1901	500 N. Third
Woodruff County	District Courthouse	CT	1902	Main Street
Sharp, J. Harry	R-nc	T&H	1918	

FITZHUGH

CLIENT	BLDG-PROJECT	ARCHITECT	DATE	ADDRESS
Sharp, Henry	R-nc	TH	1918	

HOWELL

CLIENT	BLDG-PROJECT	ARCHITECT	DATE	ADDRESS
Cole, L. L.	Comm-nc	T&H	1922	
Cole, L. L.	Store-nc	T&H	1922	

MCCRORY

CLIENT	BLDG-PROJECT	ARCHITECT	DATE	ADDRESS
Fokes Merc. Co.	Store-nc	CT	1904	
McCrory School Board	School-nc	CT	1905	
McCrory Merch. Co.	Store-nc	CT	1908	Second & Ermmonds

YELL COUNTY

DANVILLE

CLIENT	BLDG-PROJECT	ARCHITECT	DATE	ADDRESS
Danville School Board	School-nc	CT	1900	
Douglas, P. A.	R-nc	CT		
Falls, A. N.	R-nc	CT	1900-1911	

OLA

CLIENT	BLDG-PROJECT	ARCHITECT	DATE	ADDRESS
Jacoway, W. D.	R-nc	CT		

STATE: LOUISIANA

ALEXANDRIA

CLIENT	BLDG-PROJECT	ARCHITECT	DATE	ADDRESS
Lee, Mr. F. R.	R-nc	CT		

FARMERVILLE

CLIENT	BLDG-PROJECT	ARCHITECT	DATE	ADDRESS
Breed, T. J.	R-nc	CT		

LAKE PROVIDENCE

CLIENT	BLDG-PROJECT	ARCHITECT	DATE	ADDRESS
School Board Lake Providence	R-nc	G&S	1907	

MONROE

CLIENT	BLDG-PROJECT	ARCHITECT	DATE	ADDRESS
Downes, Mr. Richard, Jr.	R-nc	T&H	1919	

STATE: MISSOURI

POPLAR BLUFF

CLIENT	BLDG-PROJECT	ARCHITECT	DATE	ADDRESS
Curry, Mr. T.	R-nc	CT		

STATE: OKLAHOMA

MCALESTER

CLIENT	BLDG-PROJECT	ARCHITECT	DATE	ADDRESS
Busby, William	R			

STATE: TENNESSEE

MEMPHIS

CLIENT	BLDG-PROJECT	ARCHITECT	DATE	ADDRESS
E. L. Bruce Co.	Comm-nc	SG		
E. L. Bruce Co.	Comm-add	SG		
Goodman, Abe	R-nc	S		
Masonic Temple	Lodge-Cumberland Lodge	CT		

NASHVILLE

CLIENT	BLDG-PROJECT	ARCHITECT	DATE	ADDRESS
Masonic Temple	Lodge-Cumberland Lodge	CT	1910	

INDEX

ILLUSTRATION CREDITS

Fig. 1 Bob Dunn
Fig. 2 Tom Scott Gordon
Fig. 3 Greg Hursley
Fig. 4 Quapaw Quarter Association
Fig. 5 Quapaw Quarter Association
Fig. 6 Larry Martin, for the Quapaw Quarter Association
Fig. 7 *Plastering: Plain & Decorative,* by William Millar, 1905, from the Quapaw Quarter Association
Fig. 8 Arkansas Territorial Restoration
Fig. 9 The Cromwell Collection
Fig. 10 *1871 City Directory,* Arkansas History Commission
Fig. 11 Quapaw Quarter Association
Fig. 12 Arkansas History Commission
Fig. 13 Arkansas History Commission
Fig. 14 Quapaw Quarter Association
Fig. 15 Carl Miller, Jr. Collection, Quapaw Quarter Association
Fig. 16 The Thompson Collection, Old State House Museum
Fig. 17 *1890 City Directory,* Arkansas History Commission
Fig. 18 Arkansas History Commission
Fig. 19 Greg Hursley
Fig. 20 Tom Scott Gordon
Fig. 21 *1895 Greeting Book,* The Cromwell Collection
Fig. 22 *1895 Greeting Book,* The Cromwell Collection
Fig. 23 Arkansas History Commission
Fig. 24 Greg Hursley
Fig. 25 The Thompson Collection, Old State House Museum
Fig. 26 Christopher Lark
Fig. 27 Courtesy of Charles Witsell, Jr.
Fig. 28 Courtesy of Wilson Stiles
Fig. 29 The Thompson Collection, Old State House Museum
Fig. 30 Greg Hursley
Sidebar, page 31 Courtesy of Charles Witsell, Jr.
Fig. 31 The Thompson Collection, Old State House Museum
Fig. 32 Tom Scott Gordon
Fig. 33 Tom Scott Gordon
Fig. 34 Tom Scott Gordon
Fig. 35 The Thompson Collection, Old State House Museum
Fig. 36 The Thompson Collection, Old State House Museum
Fig. 37 The Thompson Collection, Old State House Museum
Fig. 38 The Thompson Collection, Old State House Museum

Fig. 39 The Thompson Collection, Old State House Museum
Fig. 40 Tom Scott Gordon
Fig. 41 The Thompson Collection, Old State House Museum
Fig. 42 Greg Hursley
Fig. 43 Greg Hursley
Fig. 44 Tom Scott Gordon
Fig. 45 Bob Dunn, for the Arkansas Historic Preservation Program
Fig. 46 Quapaw Quarter Association
Fig. 47 Bob Dunn, for the Arkansas Historic Preservation Program
Fig. 48 The Thompson Collection, Old State House Museum
Fig. 49 Greg Hursley
Fig. 50 The Thompson Collection, Old State House Museum
Fig. 51 Courtesy Jim Connor
Fig. 52 Bob Dunn, for the Arkansas Historic Preservation Program
Fig. 53 Tom Scott Gordon
Fig. 54 The Thompson Collection, Old State House Museum
Fig. 55 The Thompson Collection, Old State House Museum
Fig. 56 Bob Dunn, for the Arkansas Historic Preservation Program
Fig. 57 Christopher Lark
Fig. 58 Tom Scott Gordon
Fig. 59 Greg Hursley
Fig. 60 Greg Hursley
Fig. 61 Greg Hursley
Fig. 62 Tom Scott Gordon
Fig. 63 Greg Hursley
Fig. 64 Greg Hursley
Fig. 65 Christopher Lark
Fig. 66 Quapaw Quarter Association
Fig. 67 Tom Scott Gordon
Fig. 68 Greg Hursley
Fig. 69 Greg Hursley
Fig. 70 The Thompson Collection, Old State House Museum
Fig. 71 Greg Hursley
Fig. 72 Peter Tata
Fig. 73 Greg Hursley
Fig. 74 Christopher Lark
Fig. 75 The Thompson Collection, Old State House Museum
Fig. 76 Christopher Lark
Fig. 77 Christopher Lark
Fig. 78 Greg Hursley
Fig. 79 The Cromwell Collection
Fig. 80 Quapaw Quarter Association
Fig. 81 Arkansas State Capitol Association

Fig. 146 A. B. Banks gazebo, Fordyce

Fig. 82 The Cromwell Collection
Fig. 83 Greg Hursley
Fig. 84 Arkansas History Commission
Fig. 85 Greg Hursley
Fig. 86 Greg Hursley
Fig. 87 Courtesy Arlington Hotel
Fig. 88 Courtesy Mimi Dickinson
Fig. 89 Courtesy Mimi Dickinson
Fig. 90 Courtesy Mimi Dickinson
Fig. 91 Greg Hursley
Fig. 92 The Thompson Collection, Old State House Museum
Fig. 93 The Thompson Collection, Old State House Museum
Fig. 94 Greg Hursley
Fig. 95 Tom Scott Gordon
Fig. 96 Courtesy Colonel A. J. Almand
Fig. 97 The Thompson Collection, Old State House Museum
Fig. 98 Greg Hursley
Fig. 99 Greg Hursley
Fig. 100 Greg Hursley
Fig. 101 Christopher Lark
Fig. 102 Tom Scott Gordon
Fig. 103 The Thompson Collection, Old State House Museum
Fig. 104 The Thompson Collection, Old State House Museum

Sidebar, page 81 The Cromwell Collection
Fig. 105 Greg Hursley
Fig. 106 Greg Hursley
Fig. 107 Christopher Lark
Fig. 108 Christopher Lark
Fig. 109 Bob Dunn, for the Arkansas Historic Preservation Program
Fig. 110 Bob Dunn, for the Arkansas Historic Preservation Program
Fig. 111 The Cromwell Collection
Fig. 112 The Cromwell Collection
Fig. 113 Greg Hursley
Fig. 114 Greg Hursley
Fig. 115 Greg Hursley
Fig. 116 Quapaw Quarter Association
Fig. 117 Christopher Lark
Fig. 118 Greg Hursley
Fig. 119 Tom Scott Gordon
Fig. 120 Tom Scott Gordon
Fig. 121 Tom Scott Gordon
Fig. 122 Greg Hursley
Fig. 123 Tom Scott Gordon
Fig. 124 Quapaw Quarter Association
Fig. 125 Thomas Harding
Fig. 126 William Davis, for the Cromwell Firm
Fig. 127 Richard Payne, for the Cromwell Firm
Fig. 128 O. Baitz, for the Cromwell Firm
Fig. 129 Tom Scott Gordon
Fig. 130 Christopher Lark
Fig. 131 Christopher Lark
Fig. 132 Christopher Lark
Fig. 133 Christopher Lark
Fig. 134 Greg Hursley
Fig. 135 Christopher Lark
Fig. 136 Bob Dunn, for the Arkansas Historic Preservation Program
Fig. 137 Greg Hursley
Fig. 138 Bob Dunn, for the Arkansas Historic Preservation Program
Fig. 139 Christopher Lark
Fig. 140 Greg Hursley
Fig. 141 Tom Scott Gordon
Fig. 142 Greg Hursley
Fig. 143 Christopher Lark
Fig. 144 Bob Dunn, for the Arkansas Historic Preservation Program
Fig. 145 Greg Hursley
Fig. 146 Greg Hursley